WHAT WE CAN'T NOT KNOW

Praise for J. Budziszewski's

What We Can't Not Know

"Magnificent . . . an enormously important book, well-written, well-argued, and, let it be said, well-designed and printed as well. Once more, Budziszewski has put us in his debt."

Claremont Review of Books

—

"I know of no better resource for understanding the effects of sin on our contemporary culture."

Chuck Colson, *Breakpoint*

—

"A richly satisfying experience. . . . Anyone who thinks philosophy has to be dry and abstract shouldn't think so after reading Budziszewski. . . . empowering and inspiring."

Boundless webzine

—

"Superb."

Booklist

—

"Engaging style and intellectual rigor . . . *What We Can't Not Know* provides young people with the argumentative ammunition they need."

First Things

"An unabashed response to the groundless pluralistic outlook that pervades secular postmodern culture."

Religion & Liberty

—

"Aside from the sheer force of Budziszewski's argument, *What We Can't Not Know* [is] engaging."

Weekly Standard

—

"Budziszewski passionately and polemically challenges the moral shortcomings of contemporary society."

Publishers Weekly

—

"This very sophisticated book has rock-solid philosophical and theological foundations.... Budziszewski, with wit and wisdom, guides readers in relearning what we have known all along."

National Catholic Register

—

"If you want to understand the law of nature and how we know it, this is the one book to read. I wish every college student could take a course in this subject from this teacher."

PHILLIP E. JOHNSON
Jefferson E. Peyser Professor of Law Emeritus
University of California at Berkeley

"In J. Budziszewski the world has found a formidable champion of common sense—grounded in the natural order of things, joined to relentless reason, illumined by faith, and served up with wit that both devastates and elevates. *What We Can't Not Know* is a book that thinking people can't not want to read."

REV. RICHARD JOHN NEUHAUS
Editor in Chief, *First Things*

—

"J. Budziszewski shows that even the most sophisticated skeptics unwittingly reveal their moral knowledge in attempts to justify killing, lying, stealing, committing adultery, and other sins. In the very process of attacking Judaeo-Christian moral principles, they confirm them."

ROBERT P. GEORGE
McCormick Professor of Jurisprudence
Princeton University

—

"This book is very much the return of what can't be permanently repressed."

DAVID NOVAK
J. Richard and Dorothy Shiff Chair of Jewish Studies
University of Toronto

—

"This book is meant to be *thought*, not just read, and incorporated into *self*-knowledge.

MICHAEL NOVAK
George Frederick Jewett Scholar
American Enterprise Institute

"Budziszewski's gentle but incisive diagnosis of our daily evasions and rationalizations, and his excavation of the perennial truths 'we cannot not know,' reminds one of C. S. Lewis."

RUSSELL HITTINGER
Warren Professor of Catholic Studies
University of Tulsa

—

"Budziszewski's topic could not be more urgent and timely. This book needs to be pondered by everyone concerned with issues surrounding our cultural, moral, and civic life."

MICHAEL CROMARTIE
Vice President
Ethics and Public Policy Center

WHAT WE CAN'T
NOT KNOW

A Guide

J. BUDZISZEWSKI

SPENCE PUBLISHING COMPANY • DALLAS
2003

Published in the United States by
Spence Publishing Company
111 Cole Street
Dallas, Texas 75207

Library of Congress Control Number
for the hardcover edition: 2002117781

ISBN 1-890626-54-6

Printed in the United States of America

To my grandparents

Julian and Janina Budziszewski,

Long Departed,

Not Forgotten

The mind of man is the product of live Law;
it thinks by law, it dwells in the midst of law,
it gathers from law its growth; with law, therefore,
can it alone work to any result.

George MacDonald

Contents

Whom This Book Is For

The persuaded, the half-persuaded,
and the wish-I-were-persuaded

T HIS BOOK IS ABOUT THE LOST WORLD of the common truths—
about what we all really know about right and wrong. For whom
is it written? Not everyone. I am writing for the persuaded, the
half-persuaded, and the wish-I-were-persuaded. It isn't that I am not
interested in the others. But one cannot do everything at once, and at
the moment I am not trying to convert. Convincing dissenters that they
too really know what I claim they know is a task for another time, and
although I do offer a few suggestions about how to do that, it isn't what
I'm doing *here.*

Now every writer has a point of view. Mine is Christian. Some
people will wish I had not said so; we encourage people of certain per-
suasions to "come out of the closet," but Christians are supposed to stay
inside it. If they don't stay inside it, they are accused of wanting others
to get inside it. So let me make my purpose clear. In remarking that the
book is Christian I do not mean to exclude non-Christians from the
discussion, but to invite them in.

The reason for inviting them is that all people feel the weight of the moral law. Now it is true that not all people acknowledge this weight *as real law;* for that one has to believe in God, otherwise one will call it the weight of "instincts," "feelings," "socialization," or some such thing instead of law. But Christians are not the only people who acknowledge the moral law as law. We aren't even the first, for we are merely adopted children of Abraham, and the natural children were there before us. So another way to describe the audience of this book is to say that I am speaking not just to people of my own faith, but also to our older brothers, the Jews; and not only to Jews, but to all sorts of theists and would-be theists. When other people write of the common truths, naturally they will do so from within their own traditions. Rabbi David Novak, for example, has written about them from within Judaism.[1] Whenever they do so, I will be grateful for their voice, as I am for his.

In this book I hope to achieve two things. The first is bolster the confidence of plain people in the rational foundations of their common moral sense. This requires not only explaining what these rational foundations are, but also explaining why this common sense is under attack— in particular, explaining how it is even *possible* for what we all really know to be denied, and why this *doesn't* mean that isn't really known.

The second goal is to present the explanation in such a way that all of the people who think and write about the common truths can achieve a firmer alliance in their defense. The object of such an alliance is to do what this book doesn't do—to address the uncertain, the disoriented, and the self-deceived among our neighbors in a way which may bring them back into the fold of moral sense and sanity.

Unfortunately, the traditions which do affirm the common truths speak in such different ways that the unanimity of this affirmation is obscured. One group speaks of the Noahide Commandments, another of Common Grace, another of Natural Law. Jews think "natural law" is a Christian thing, Protestants think it is a Catholic thing, and Catholics sometimes think it a medieval thing. In medieval times, some people thought that it was a Roman thing, and in Roman times, some people thought that it was a Stoic thing. On the contrary, by whatever name it is called it is a shared thing, a human thing, and most of the various traditions and theories about it hold similar presuppositions.

So, although I write from a Christian perspective, I try to keep these shared presuppositions in view. It isn't that I don't comment on the insights contributed by my own faith; I do, at some length. But I distinguish these insights from the shared presuppositions. My hope is not that we will never criticize or challenge each other, but that when we do, our challenges will become more constructive. To maintain a common moral front despite our disagreements about even deeper matters— such deeper disagreements as how to be *restored* to the bosom of that God whom we all claim to acknowledge—we need to talk with, not past, each other.

To return to the question of the audience. "The persuaded, the half-persuaded, and those desirous of being persuaded about the common moral truths, not only Christians, but also Jews, and not only Jews, but all sorts of theists and would-be theists": although that is a broad category, it is obviously not universal, especially in our own times. Perhaps you who are reading this preface are committed to the other side. If you are—if you are firmly convinced that you *don't* really know what I claim we all really know—if you are not merely uncertain, but in opposition— let me say a word to you too.

Obviously you are not a part of my expected audience. But that does not mean that I want to hide the book from you; you are welcome to be a fly on the wall and listen in. Nor does it mean that I do not want to talk with you; this particular book is not a good vehicle of that hoped-for conversation, but by all means let us talk. But let us be honest too. We *are* on different sides.

Some people consider it "uncivil" to say so. They think the "culture war" is the fault of people who admit there is a culture war, and that the very use of terms like "culture war" demonizes people on the other side.

In their view, we must pretend that we all want the same things. But we don't all want the same things, do we? We don't even frame the issues in the same way. To mention but a single issue, I say that I want to protect life, but you say that I want to oppose choice. What I call life you call anti-choice, and what you call choice I call killing.

I wish that this were only a quibble over words. There are few greater disagreements than the meaning of life and death, and it isn't easy to see how people who disagree about it can agree about much else—at least much else of importance. In this conflict and bewilderment, and in all the related conflicts about the other great questions of how to live, to die, and to live together, some people use diplomacy itself as a means of war (I deplore the fact, but it is true), and what some people call "civility" is less about true civility than about making fools of the opposition. I believe in civility. But it is not a requirement of civility to pretend that there is no war.

Please understand me. If you truly reject the truths I say we "can't not know," I do consider you desperately confused, as, probably, you consider me. Moreover, I believe, not just from theory but from experience, that to be confused about such fundamental things, one must deeply want to be—for I was once on your side too, and I have given a lot of thought to how I got there and to why I stayed so long. But to speak of the embattlement of the public square does not mean that I hate you, that I have contempt for you, or that I consider my own side pure. On the contrary, one of the slogans of the folk on my side of the argument is that "All men sin and fall short of the glory of God." "All" includes us too. That means the quarrel is not between sinners and innocents, but between sinners who confess the moral facts which accuse us all, and sinners who deny them. But of course "sin" is another of those "uncivil" words.

"Why can't we all just get along?" One reason is that we are no longer in ordinary times, when people more or less agree about the basic norms for human life (even if they violate them), but disagree about their implications. We are in extraordinary times, when people contend about the basic norms themselves. And how shall such dispute be conducted, when the norms for dispute are among the norms disputed? That is what our times are finding out.

As I said at the beginning, one cannot do everything at once, and I am not, in this book, seeking to draw those on the far side over to the near one. Even so, if you are over there, I would like to draw you. If you would like to come, I would love to have you back. In the meantime— so far as you will accept it—peace.

ACKNOWLEDGMENTS

Bits and pieces of what became this book have appeared previously in *First Things, The American Journal of Juriprudence,* and *World,* for whose pages and courtesies I am most grateful. For the opportunity to discuss or present portions of the argument at various meetings, and for the ideas there exchanged, I am much in debt, especially at the conferences "Crime and Punishment," School of Law, University of Notre Dame; "Disputed Questions: Contemporary Controversies Concerning Aquinas," Department of Medieval and Renaissance Studies, New York University; "The Foundations of Law," Trinity Evangelical Divinity School; various informal meetings at the Ethics and Public Policy Center; and the working group on "The Nature of the Human Person," sponsored by the Pew Charitable Trusts.

Especially do I thank all those with whom I have the pleasure of conversation at one time or another on natural law or related subjects: Hadley Arkes, Christopher Beem, Michael J. Behe, Iain Benson, Peter Berkowitz, Joseph Bottum, Gerard V. Bradley, Harold O.J. Brown, Michael Budde, Eloise Buker, Francis Canavan, Nigel M. de Sales Cameron, Ernesto Caparros, Daniel Cere, Jonathan Chaplin, the late David Orgon Coolidge, Jesse Cougle, Alan R. Crippen, Michael

Cromartie, Fred Dallmayr, William A. Dembski, David K. DeWolf, John DiIulio, Darrell Dobbs, Jean Bethke Elshtain, Carl H. Esbeck, John Finnis, Norman L. Geisler, Robert P. George, Kenneth L. Grasso, Bruce W. Green, Germain G. Grisez, Jeanne Heffernan, John P. Hittinger, Russell Hittinger, Phillip E. Johnson, Diane L. Knippers, Robert C. Koons, Joseph W. Koterski, Dorothy McCartney, Michael McConnell, Timothy and Lydia McGrew, Dan Manengo, Joshua Mitchell, Siobhan Nash-Marshall, David Naugle, Richard John Neuhaus, Joseph and Linda Nicolosi, David Novak, Michael Novak, Edward T. Oakes, Marvin Olasky, Susan Orr, J.I. Packer, Keith J. Pavlischek, Nancy Pearcey, John A. Perricone, Jeff Peterson, Mike Potemra, James V. Schall, James L. Siebach, William Stevenson, Herb and Terry Schlossberg, Frank Slade, John G. Stackhouse, Phillip Thompson, Michael Uhlmann, Paul Vitz, Peter Wehner, John West, W. Bradford Wilcox, Albert M. Wolters, Christopher Wolfe, the participants in Phylogeny, and innumerable others, whose names would fill another book.

To my wife Sandra I owe myself many times over, as no doubt she knows, though she never lets on. Or not very often.

It seems to me that every writer should end with gratitude to the one who was in the beginning, and whose very name is Word. A reviewer—a friendly one—once remarked that it seemed strange to see that sort of thanks in a book, as though the author were claiming divine inspiration. Of course, for whatever is amiss in these pages (and there will be much), the blame is mine. But permit me to be grateful if anything in them is true.

WHAT WE CAN'T NOT KNOW

The Moral Common Ground

*The foundational moral principles are not only
right for all, but at some level known to all.*

ONCE UPON A TIME it was possible for a philosopher to write that
the foundational moral principles are "the same for all, both
as to rectitude and as to knowledge"[1]—and expect everyone
to agree. To say that these principles are the same for all "as to rectitude" means that they are right for everyone; in other words, deliberately taking innocent human life, sleeping with my neighbor's wife, and
mocking God are as wrong for me as they are for you, no matter what
either of us believes. To say that they are the same for all "as to knowledge" means that at some level, everyone knows them; even the murderer knows the wrong of murder, the adulterer the wrong of adultery,
the mocker the wrong of mockery. He may say that he doesn't, but he
does. There are no real moral skeptics; supposed skeptics are playing
make-believe, and doing it badly.

As I say, once upon a time a thinker who wrote such words could
expect nearly everyone to agree. And nearly everyone did. The Christians agreed, the Jews agreed, and the Muslims agreed. Moreover, they

could call to their support the consensus of the rest of the human race. One might search the wide world over for a people who did not know the moral basics, but one would fail.

To be sure, the wide world over people also carved out excuses for themselves. I must not take innocent human life—but only my tribe is human. I must not sleep with my neighbor's wife—but I can make my neighbor's mine. I must not mock deity—but I can ascribe deity to a created thing instead of the Creator. And so, not only was moral knowledge universal, but the determination to play tricks on moral knowledge was universal, too. A law was written on the heart of man, but it was everywhere entangled with the evasions and subterfuges of men. Even so that law endured; and even so it was seen to endure.

IS THERE NO COMMON GROUND?

Today all that has changed. A thinker who writes such words can no longer expect most people to agree. In fact he must expect most people to disagree. He will be told that the foundational moral principles are plainly *not* the same for all, probably not even as to rectitude, and certainly not as to knowledge. They may not even be right for all, and they are certainly not known to all.

For example, don't we disagree profoundly about all three of the great matters I mentioned above—death, sex, and God? Consider death. An entire generation has now come of age taking for granted the liberty to kill one's children in the dim, soft refuge which was once considered the safest of all: the womb. The latest social movements seek to extend this strange liberty to other sorts of killing, especially infanticide and euthanasia. Whereas once it was thought that the helpless had the greatest claim on our protection, now it is held that they have the least. Most medical schools have rewritten the Hippocratic oath to accommodate the view that a physician may be a killer as well as healer.

Rather than ringing alarms about such changes, professional "ethicists" are in the front ranks of their promoters. A good example is found in the influential British bioethicist Jonathan Glover. According to this expert, human beings do not have a "right" to life at all. Personhood, he holds, is a matter of degree; some humans have more of it than others. He says that even some of those who do rate as persons have lives not worth living. One recalls the phrase of the early German euthanasia promoters, *lebensunwerten Leben*—"life unworthy of life"—but Glover goes yet further. Even the weak principle "it is wrong to destroy a life *which is worth living*" is too strong for him, for he says one must consider other values, and "there is a tacit 'other things being equal' clause." Occasionally it may even be right to kill someone who is not dying and who wants to go on living. He does say that only a monster of self-confidence would feel no qualms about such an act. Unfortunately, he does not say that only a monster of self-confidence would commit it. For people who do feel squeamish, he has advice: If you are going to kill, then use means that have other desirable effects. For example, you might deliberately administer an excessive dose of painkiller. This "has the advantage of perhaps being less distressing to the person who has to carry it out"—and it has a "blurring quality which makes prosecution less likely."

Abortion and infanticide are easier still. In Glover's view, neither of these acts is "directly" or intrinsically wrong. Abortion should be permitted at any stage, for any reason—even a late abortion because the parents want a boy, or because the mother's pregnancy "will prevent a holiday abroad." After all, he says, unborn babies are "replaceable." So, for that matter, are born ones: "if the mother will have other children instead, it is not directly wrong to prevent *this* foetus or baby from surviving." You can always have a better one later. Infanticide he sees as a slightly different case, but only because killing born babies has stronger effects on third parties than killing unborn babies does. For example, it upsets people more. And it is more likely to set the culture on a slippery slope (as though we weren't on one already). Although Glover considers the side effects of abortion too slight to justify *any* limits, he concedes that the side effects of infanticide may be great enough to justify *some* limits. But side effects can be reduced, and he offers suggestions for reducing the side effects of abortions. For example, if performing them does make abortionists and their helpers feel distress, then we could regard these people as "especially heroic, doing something intrinsically distasteful which yet prevents much unhappiness." That would make them feel better. I suppose something like this could also be arranged for the people who work in infanticide centers. Then more infanticides could be allowed.

Notice the assumption behind all of this. We make up our foundational moral principles as we go along. They are not a given, like the laws of arithmetic, but a product of culture, like the style of our architecture. If we don't like them, we can make up new ones. Traditional principles about the sanctity of human life and the horror of taking it from innocents may therefore be discarded when we have no further use for them; they don't reflect authentic moral knowledge. They represent what *previous* people have invented, and if we would rather invent something different, we may. As Glover puts it: "The prospects of reviving belief in a moral law are dim. Looking for an external validation of morality is less effective than building breakwaters. Morality could be abandoned, or it can be re-created. It may survive in a more defensible form when seen to be a human creation. We can shape it consciously to serve people's needs and interests, and to reflect the things we most care about."[2]

Notice too what follows if Glover's assumption is accepted. He says that "we" can re-create morality to suit ourselves. But who is this "we"? Presumably, people like Glover. But there are other people. If morality is created, not discovered, then surely different groups and individuals will create *different* moralities, for they will "care most" about different things. There will be no common standard by which to adjudicate the conflicts among these invented moralities. The clashes among them will be like clashes of clothing styles, with this strange difference—that the stakes are who lives and who dies.

This is just the quandary in which Glover finds himself. To be sure, he says that there are "resources," like sympathy and respect, on which the creators of morality might draw. But as his own sources tell him, the creators of other moralities may draw on other quite different resources. For some men, destruction is an intoxicant, mass murder a doorway to ecstasy, and communal killing "the closest thing to what childbirth is for women: the initiation into the power of life and death."[3] If he is right about the moral law, we have no common ground; it is merely my morality against yours.

Could it be that only intellectuals think like this? Even if that were true, it would be quite enough to worry about, because intellectuals like Glover now command the heights of the professions, the academy, the courts, and the civil service. But intellectuals are not the only ones who think like this. They are merely the ones who think like this for a living. The universal common sense is less and less *our* common sense; disbelief in a common moral ground is becoming a pillar of middle class prejudice. People still, in some fashion, believe that it is wrong to murder, wrong to steal, wrong to cheat—wrong not for them but for everyone. But "my morality, your morality" is the language of everyday life, and the reigning platitude is, "You shall not impose your morality on anyone else."

If ever a value were destined for transvaluation, surely that one is. The recent string of public school shootings are a sign of this. We are beginning to see what happens when it occurs to the children of this middle class that even the prohibition of firing shotguns at one's classmates "imposes a morality"—that the very platitude that one shall *not* impose his morality "imposes a morality." The new norm is "You may impose whatever you want to, on whomever you please, for whatever reason captures your imagination." As the adolescent mass murderer Eric Harris boasted at his website, "My belief is that if I say something, it goes. I am the law, if you don't like it, you die."

Some people think that there was once a common moral ground, but that it isn't there any longer. Many go further. They say that there *never was* a common moral ground—that the notion of a standard of right and wrong which all can share has *always* been an illusion, an illusion from which we are only now beginning to escape.

As to where the illusion came from, theories are legion. At one extreme are those who blame the illusion on biology. "Morality . . . is merely an adaptation put in place to further our reproductive ends," say Michael Ruse and E. O. Wilson. "Ethics as we understand it is an illusion fobbed off on us by our genes to get us to co-operate."[4] It is rather mysterious why Ruse and Wilson think escaping the illusion so important. It is even more mysterious how they expect anyone to escape it, considering that they suppose it to be programmed in our genes and hard-wired in our central nervous systems.

At the other extreme are those who blame the illusion on grammar. Yes, on grammar. A long chain of analytical philosophers maintains that moral questions—"Is murder always wrong?"—may *seem* to mean something because they follow the grammatical rules for the construction of meaningful sentences, but on closer examination mean nothing at all. They are "pseudo-questions" like "Does green smell worse than red?" True, the dismissal of moral questions as pseudo-questions has become somewhat less fashionable over the past couple of decades. This dismissal began to go out of style just around the time that philosophers of modest means discovered that they could make quite a good living as "practical ethicists," providing intellectual cover to businesses and hospitals and the like. Ironically, the turn to practical ethics merely deepens the sense that there is no common moral ground—because every practical ethicist gives different answers to the basic moral questions.

Yet these different answers are not completely different. The practical ethicists do have this in common, that nearly all of them oppose what *used* to be called morality. Each has his own pet principles—his own theory—and theory rules.

A case in point: Peter Singer, Ira B. DeCamp professor of bioethics at the University Center for Human Values, Princeton University, touted by the *New Yorker* as "the most influential living philosopher" and by former Princeton president Harold T. Shapiro, chairman of the National Bioethics Advisory Commission under former President Clinton, as "the most influential ethicist alive."[5] Singer's theory is utilitarianism. Its pet principle is that pleasure is the only thing with moral value; seeking pleasure and avoiding pain, the only thing that matters. But animals feel pleasure too, he observes. Some animals may even have greater capacity for pleasure than some humans. A variety of consequences follow. He says cattle should not be killed for the pleasure of diners, because it hurts the cattle. He says defective babies *may* be killed for the pleasure of their parents, because babies don't feel much anyway, and because defective people don't contribute much pleasure to society. He says a human being may have sex with a calf, but only so long as both enjoy it. But he says a human being should not have sex with a chicken, because it usually kills the chicken.[6] Everywhere the ceremony of innocence is drowned.

THERE IS A COMMON GROUND

But there is a common moral ground. Certain moral truths really are common to all human beings. Because our shoes are wet with evasions the common ground may seem slippery to us, but it is real; we do all know that we shouldn't murder, shouldn't steal, should honor our parents, should honor God, and so on. Preposterous, I know. Detail and defense of this outrageous claim are presented later in the book. The reason for writing it is just that the claim *has* become outrageous—in the original sense of provoking outrage. People become angry when one asserts the moral law.

This outrage is itself an amazing fact. It needs to be explained. Although I think that an explanation can be provided, the explanation does nothing to diminish the strangeness of the thing explained. We are passing through an eerie phase of history in which the things that everyone really knows are treated as unheard-of doctrines, a time in which the elements of common decency are themselves attacked as indecent. Nothing quite like this has ever happened before. Although our civilization has passed through quite a few troughs of immorality, never before has vice held the high *moral* ground. Our time considers it dirty-minded to treat sexual purity as a virtue; unfeeling to insist too firmly that the sick should not be encouraged to seek death; a sign of impious pride to profess humble faith in God. The moral law has become the very emblem of immorality. We call affirming it "being judgmental" and "being intolerant," which is our way of saying that it has been judged and will not be tolerated.

We should not be too discouraged. Like crabgrass growing through the cracks and crannies of concrete slabs, the awareness of the moral law breaks even through the crust of our denials. Consider Jonathan Glover again.

What makes Glover's case intriguing is that after a career opening doors to atrocity, he wishes to be thought of as one who bars the doors against them. The most recent of his books is a critique of the holocausts and gulags of the twentieth century, of their torments and monstrosities both large and small.[7] The laudable purpose of the book is to understand how ordinary people can commit terrible deeds, and how they might be prevented from committing them. Glover says he has been thinking about the problem for years. In a slip that would have done Freud proud, he adds that the relevance of his previous books[8] to the problem is "obvious"; for so it is, although not in the way that he means.

His sliding scales of personhood, his replaceable babies, his lives not worth living—these embody the same techniques of "depersonalization" and "emotional distancing" which so disturb him when they are practiced by other people. Psychologists speak of a "Stockholm Syndrome," in which victims come to identify with their captors. Perhaps there is a parallel syndrome, in which scholars of atrocity adopt some of the patterns of thinking of their subjects. Or perhaps the syndrome we are witnessing is preemptive capitulation: If we reduce our conscience to rubble before the bad men get here, they will have nothing to destroy.

But I think that the problem is deeper. Glover sees himself as replacing traditional moral principles with a morality "less likely to be eroded." The reason he thinks manmade morality more durable is that he cannot take seriously the idea of morality coming from God. A wise God, he thinks, would not have ordained a world "in which people are hanged after spending their last night nailed by the ear to a fence, or in which babies are cut out of their mothers' wombs with daggers." A wise God would have *made* man good, or at least made him grow better over time. There is a problem with this line of reasoning. It is hard to see why Glover should object to a world in which babies are cut out of their mothers' wombs with daggers, but not one in which mothers invite daggers into their wombs that their babies may be cut out. And that is only the beginning of his incoherencies. The whole meaning of morality is a rule that we ought to obey whether we like it or not. If so, then the idea of creating a morality we like better is incoherent. Moreover, it would seem that until we *had* created our new morality, we would have no standard by which to criticize God. Since we have not yet created one, the standard by which we judge Him must be the very standard that He gave us. If it is good enough to judge Him by, then why do we need a new one? Now any thinker can commit an error in logic. Multiple, matted incoherencies, like Glover's, seem to call for a different explanation. When, despite considerable intelligence, a thinker cannot think straight, it becomes very likely that he cannot face his thoughts.

The closer to the starting point his swerve, the more likely this explanation becomes. Somewhere in his mind lies a mystery of knowledge which he must hide from himself at all costs. If he presupposes the old morality in the very act of denying it, the lesson is not that the old morality should be denied, but that he is in denial. If he makes humanity God and yet cries out against God's inhumanity, it is clear who has really been accused.

The form of the indictment is *not* "If you deny P, then you are in denial about P." One is not "in denial" just because he denies that ice is cold, or that dogs normally have four legs. He might merely be mistaken; he might never have felt ice or seen dogs. Put right, the form of the indictment is "If your objection to P presupposes P, then you have not given us any grounds to disbelieve P; rather, you have given us grounds to think that you know P after all." Perhaps the older thinkers were correct after all. Perhaps the foundational moral principles really are the same for all not only as to rectitude but as to knowledge. Perhaps they really are not only right for all, but somehow known to all.

That is the claim of this book. The common moral truths are no less plain to us today than they ever were. Our problem is not that there isn't a common moral ground, but that we would rather stand somewhere else. We are not in Dante's inferno, where even the sinners acknowledge the law which they have violated. We are in some other hell. The denizens of our hell say that they don't know the law—or that there is no law—or that each makes the law for himself.

And they all know better.

THE NAME OF THE COMMON GROUND

"Common moral ground" is a cumbersome term for the foundational principles of morality, and also a little thin. Paul spoke of "a law written on the heart." That is more evocative, but too narrow; Paul wasn't referring to all the modes of moral knowledge, but only to conscience.[9]

Aristotle spoke of the "first principles of practical reason." That doesn't quite serve our purposes either, because it refers only to the axioms (so to speak) and not the theorems. In our language, the simplest, most general, and most widely used term for what I am talking about is "natural law." It takes in both the foundational moral principles and their first few rings of implications, whether known to reason through conscience or through some other means.

The term does carry baggage. Many people disbelieve in the natural law because they mix it up with some detested *theory* of the natural law, which is like disbelieving in the laws of England because one finds fault with Blackstone's famous commentaries on the laws of England. Or they mix up the natural law with a theory of something altogether unrelated to natural law, for instance the theory of "justification by works"—the idea that if only a sinner performs enough moral deeds, God will take him back. Since I began writing about natural law, opinions have been attributed to me which I would never dream of propounding, and I have been pulled into disputes which I had never dreamt of entering. Among theologians there may be found a school of thought called presuppositionalism, which in some of its forms seems to deny the natural law. A theologian once remarked to me that he liked a book I had written because it was "about time someone went after the presuppositionalists." Some time later, a philosopher wrote to complain that he *didn't* like the book because it was plain to him that I *was* a presuppositionalist. The truth is that I am not a presuppositionalist—but neither was I "going after" those who are. C. S. Lewis was so anxious to avoid such misunderstandings that he experimented with another term for natural law, borrowing from the East the term "Tao," which means "the Way." The experiment, unfortunately, was unsuccessful. Although his book *The Abolition of Man* is perhaps the greatest work on natural law in the twentieth century, most scholars of natural law have never heard of it, and quite a few people who do read it mistakenly suppose that he endorsed the Eastern philosophy of Taoism.

My own approach is to go ahead and use the suspect term "natural law," but warn readers not to jump to conclusions. In that spirit I offer the following clarifications.

Our subject is called natural *law* because it has the qualities of all law. Law has rightly been defined as an ordinance of reason, for the common good, made by him who has care of the community, and promulgated. Consider the natural law against murder. It is not an arbitrary whim, but a rule which the mind can grasp as right. It serves not some special interest, but the universal good. Its author has care of the universe, for He created it. And it is not a secret rule, for He has so arranged His creation that every rational being knows about it.

Our subject is called *natural* law because it is built into the design of human nature[10] and woven into the fabric of the normal human mind. Another reason for calling it natural is that we rightly take it to be about what really is—a rule like the prohibition of murder reflects not a mere illusion or projection, but genuine knowledge. It expresses the actual moral character of a certain kind of act.

The natural law is *not* "innate," for we are not born knowing it—although as soon as the child is capable of understanding what is meant by "murder" and by "wrong," he is capable of recognizing that murder, in fact, is wrong. The natural law is *not* mere biological instinct—although it does take account of certain biological realities, for the practical requirements of love in the context of family life would no doubt be somewhat different among beings who had only one sex or whose young were ready to assume the responsibilities of adulthood as soon as they hatched out. The natural law is *not* mere custom—although the customs of almost all times and places more or less acknowledge it. The natural law is *not* just a deceptive name for moral law as known through the Bible—although biblical moral law acknowledges it, conforms to it, and extends it. The natural law is *not* the same as the theories that philosophers construct about it—rather it is the reality which the theories attempt, with greater or lesser success, to describe. And the natural law is *not* a law of nature in the same sense that gravitation is a law of nature—indeed, principles like gravitation are "laws" only by distant analogy, for a falling apple is not freely and rationally conforming its behavior to a rule which it knows to be right.

To summarize: Certain moral principles are not only right for all, but at some level known to all. They are the universal common sense of the human race, as well as the foundation of its uncommon sense. It makes a difference that they are right for all; otherwise there would be nothing for moral reasoning and persuasion to be about. It makes a difference that they are known to all; otherwise, even though moral reasoning and persuasion would be about something, they could never get started.

To penetrate the unknown, the mind must begin with what is known already. George Orwell wrote that "We have now sunk to a depth at which re-statement of the obvious is the first duty of intelligent men." This book is an attempt at re-statement.

PART I

THE LOST WORLD

The lost treasury of ordinary sense,
and the state of the natural law tradition.

Things We Can't Not Know

*To recognize what we can't not know, we may
have to forget a few things we were taught.*

ERE IS THE ARGUMENT SO FAR. However rude it may be these days to say so, there are some moral truths that we all really know—truths which a normal human being is unable *not* to know. They are a universal possession, an emblem of rational mind, an heirloom of the family of man. That doesn't mean that we know them with unfailing perfect clarity, or that we have reasoned out their remotest implications: we don't, and we haven't. Nor does it mean that we never pretend not to know them even though we do, or that we never lose our nerve when told they aren't true: we do, and we do. It doesn't even mean that we are born knowing them, that we never get mixed up about them, or that we assent to them just as readily whether they are taught to us or not. *That* can't even be said of "two plus two is four." Yet our common moral knowledge is as real as arithmetic, and probably just as plain. Paradoxically, maddeningly, we appeal to it even to justify wrongdoing; rationalization is the homage paid by sin to guilty knowledge.

These basic moral principles, together with their first few rings of implications, are the natural law. That may sound easy, but now comes work. Because the heart is devious, the hardest work is simply facing them. Because the world is complicated, the next-hardest is applying them. For both these reasons, we make theories about the natural law, and also for a third—to oblige our sense of awe. I mean, of course, that these are the good reasons for theorizing. There are bad ones too.

AS REAL AS ARITHMETIC?

If there are truths that we can't not know, and others, perhaps, that we can't help learning, then what are they? Let's begin with what mankind grasps even in the midst of his evasions—that is to say, not precisely with what we really know, which is quite a lot, but with what the great majority of us in all times and places admit that we know, which is rather less. I like this old summary, offered by John M. Cooper in 1931:

> The peoples of the world, however much they differ as to details of morality, hold universally, or with practical universality, to at least the following basic precepts. Respect the Supreme Being or the benevolent being or beings who take his place. Do not "blaspheme." Care for your children. Malicious murder or maiming, stealing, deliberate slander or "black" lying, when committed against friend or unoffending fellow clansman or tribesman, are reprehensible. Adultery proper is wrong, even though there be exceptional circumstances that permit or enjoin it and even though sexual relations among the unmarried may be viewed leniently. Incest is a heinous offense. This universal moral code agrees rather closely with our own Decalogue taken in a strictly literal sense.[1]

Cooper's reminder was lost among those other travelers' tales of Pacific free-love paradises and African tribes devoid of conscience. But Margaret Mead was wrong about the Samoans, and Colin Turnbull was wrong about the Ik; the former turned out to be fierce defenders of chastity, the latter to have a strong sense of mutual obligation. Like other people, anthropologists may see only what they want to see, even when what they want to see is nothing.

Interestingly, a part of the common moral sense is that there *is* a common moral sense. It is not only a recurring theme in philosophy, but a tradition in most cultures and a presupposition of both Jewish and Christian scriptures. Philosophers call this common sense the "natural" law to convey the idea that it is somehow rooted in how things really are. Chinese wisdom traditions call it the Tao; Indian, the dharma or rita. The Talmud says it was given to the "sons" or descendants of Noah, which means all of us. Abraham was so sure of it that he dared to debate with God. Paul said that when gentiles do by nature what the law requires, they show that its works are "written on their hearts."

Thinkers concoct controversial theories about the plain man's moral understanding, theories in which the plain man takes no interest and which he does not understand. Yet even then, the plain man's knowledge constrains them. Short of direct divine revelation, there is simply no other place for moral reflection to begin, no other place for the wise to get their data. Good moral philosophers therefore don't announce postulates that make no sense to anyone but themselves; rather, they connect the dots of what we know already and bring repressed or latent knowledge to the surface. Consider Cooper's summary again. Although it may be difficult for my will to move from loving my tribesman as myself to loving a stranger as myself, it is no great leap for the understanding; the Sinaitic tribes even grouped the two maxims nearby (Leviticus 19:18 and 19:34), showing that the question "Who is my neighbor?" was ancient even then. An equally short intellectual distance separates the widespread negative form of the Golden Rule from the positive: "Do not do unto others as you would not be done by" from "Do unto them as you would be." Again, if taking my neighbor's wife is so gravely wrong, then it isn't hard to work out that I should never do it. From not having my neighbor's wife to not desiring her is a pretty small step as well, and

if conjugal union is so singular and set apart, then it isn't difficult to see
the parallel between sex against it and sex before. Concerning "the be-
nevolent being or beings" who take God's place, it is remarkable how
widespread among pagan peoples we find the tradition of a High God
above and beyond the lesser ones, even though He may not be offered
any oblations.[2] Against this background, Paul's complaint that the pagans are not ignorant of God, but rather ignore Him (Romans 1:18-21),
makes good sense.

Even poor moral philosophy tries to connect the dots of what we
know already; the problem is that it does so badly. It picks and chooses
which dots to connect, "cooking" the moral data as an incompetent stat-
istician cooks the numbers. For example, we like to feel pleasure, so the
utilitarian sort of cook ignores every datum but that. As utilitarians
would have it, we don't want dinner, but the pleasure of feeling full; nor
knowledge, but the pleasure of feeling knowledgeable; nor love, but the
pleasure of feeling loved; nor God, but the pleasure of feeling—well,
whatever God makes one feel. It follows that if it were possible to have
the pleasures without the things, that would be just as good: Eat, purge,
and eat again. But why even go to that much trouble? Why not just shoot
electricity into our pleasure centers and be done with it? A glucose and
vitamin tap could keep us alive; only enough consciousness would be
needed to be conscious of pleasure itself. Turn out the lights when you
leave, Doctor. Thank you. Good night.

After decades of being lectured to by various groups—utilitarians
(who ignore every dot but pleasure), libertarians (who ignore every dot
but rights), relativists (who let everyone make up his own dots)—we
are hearing from natural lawyers again. Why now?

Partly because we need the authentic natural law to save us from its
impersonators. When the Supreme Court announced a "right to define
one's own concept of existence, of meaning, of the universe, and of the
mystery of human life,"[3] some thought it was rejecting the very idea of
natural law. Really it was asserting a degenerate theory of natural law,

one widely held in the culture—or at least in those parts of it which our controllers choose to recognize, such as law schools, abortion facilities, and liberal seminaries. It was propounding a universal moral right *not* to recognize the universal moral laws on which all rights depend. Such liberty has infinite length but zero depth. A right is a power to make a moral claim upon me. If I could "define" your claims into nonexistence—as the Court said I could "define" the unborn child's—that power would be destroyed.

Can we turn back the clock? Like John Bunyan's pilgrim, can we return to the place where we got off the track and get back onto it again? Can we open the shuttered windows and let in the light of natural law?

Making good on this claim requires an understanding of nature as *designed* according to certain purposes. We have to view every kind of thing there is as an arrow directed naturally to its goal. The way St. Thomas put this was to say that the "nature" of any particular thing is "a purpose, implanted by the Divine Art, that it be moved to a determinate end." Provided that we haven't been taught not to, this is the way we tend to think of things anyway. An acorn is not *essentially* something small with a point at one end and a cap at the other; it is something aimed at being an oak. A boy in my neighborhood is not *essentially* something with baggy pants and a foul mouth; he is something aimed at being a man. In this way of thinking, everything in Creation is a wannabe. We just have to recognize what it naturally wants to be. Natural law turns out to be the developmental spec sheet, the guide for getting there. For the acorn, nature isn't law in the strictest sense, because law must be addressed to an intelligent being capable of choice. For the boy, though, it is. The acorn can't be in conflict with itself. He can.

But there is something missing here. According to the old tradition of natural law, the human arrow is unlike all others because it is directed to a goal which its natural powers cannot reach. We have one natural longing that nothing in nature can satisfy. That boy on the corner is something that by nature wants to be a Man, and being a Man is hard enough. But a Man is something that by nature wants to be in friendship with God, and that, short of grace, is impossible. God is not only the author of human nature, but the direction in which it faces and the power on which it depends, its greatest good. He isn't just the most important good *for me* because of my faith commitments; He is the most important simply. Revealed religion concurs. "For [even] the Gentiles seek all these things; and your heavenly Father knows that you need them all. But seek first His kingdom and His righteousness, and all these things shall be yours as well."

Suddenly we run into a massive problem, for now we are speaking of two laws, the natural and the divine. The God who implanted His law in our design upsets the boat by announcing another law in words. What a scandal! Embarrassed, some natural lawyers assure us that the natural law would make perfect sense even if there were no God at all— forgetting that if there were no God there would be no nature either. On the other hand, some believers say that since we have the Bible to tell us what to do, we don't need a natural law.

To such folk I may seem to be in trouble, because in the rest of this chapter and the next I will be drawing in some detail from Jewish and Christian scriptures and from Christian reflections about them. The charge will be that I am plainly not speaking about the natural law, but only about the particular teachings of my own religion, and the demand will be that if I am serious about discussing the natural law, I must discuss the generic, not the particular. After all, haven't I claimed that the natural law concerns what is not only right for all, but known to all?

APOLOGION

I'm sorry, but moral knowledge doesn't work that way; to say much about the generic one *has* to speak of the particular. Even though the elementary principles of the moral law are known by nature, they are elicited, elucidated, and elaborated by tradition. The notion that it could be otherwise expresses not the classical view of natural law, but a modern distortion of the classical view which took hold only in the Enlightenment. This distortion led to such silliness that eventually serious people gave up on natural law altogether.

Nature dependent on tradition—does this sound inconsistent? It shouldn't. Even insights into "what we can't not know" require the assistance of others, for a good deal of what we know is latent: we may not realize *what it is* that we know, and we are certainly unlikely to know all its presuppositions and implications. Most of the "others" on whose assistance we rely will belong to previous generations, because people of our own time are likely to have the same blind spots that we do. What sound tradition does for us is like what some sculptors say they do with the marble: liberate the figure which is imprisoned in the block. It gives voice to what in some sense we already know, but inarticulately. When tradition is silenced, people have to work all these things out for themselves—and that is impossible. There is such a thing as self-evidence, but it should never be mistaken for what is evident to the isolated self.

A second reason why we need the help of tradition is that intellect and moral character work together; if the mind is like the eyes, then the virtues are like the lenses which focus them. The classical natural law thinkers held that although there are broad moral truths which cannot be blotted out of the heart of man, there are others, more remote from first principles, which can all too easily be blotted out—and the usual way to blot them is bad living. The goods of fidelity, for example, are plain and concrete to the man who has not strayed, but they are faint, like mathematical abstractions, to the one who is addicted to other men's wives. An old-fashioned way of putting this is that the assistance of "second nature" is needed for nature to come into its own; the natural is brought to bear by the habitual. Indispensable is a living tradition which transmits not only teachings, but disciplines.

There is another problem, too, which shows that we need not only the assistance of tradition, but the assistance of a particular kind of tradition. Clear vision of the moral law is crushing. Why is that? Because the first thing that an honest man sees with this clear vision is a debt which exceeds anything he can pay. Apart from an assurance that the debt can somehow be forgiven, such honesty is too much for us; it kills. The difficulty is that without a special revelation from the Author of the law, it is impossible to know whether the possibility of forgiveness is real. Therefore we look away; unable to accept the truth about ourselves, we may keep the law in the corner of our eye, but we cannot gaze upon it steadily. We need another tradition, *greater* than natural law tradition, which settles the matter of forgiveness once and for all; otherwise our highest ethics will be cross-eyed with evasions. Why then should it be surprising that although natural law was named by the pagans and is in some dim fashion known apart from the Bible, reflection about it has never gone far except within the biblical traditions?

Paradoxically, then, even the appeal to the generic presupposes the particular; for insight into what we hold in common, we must fall back on what we do not hold in common. To say "You must not speak except generically" is to say "The most important things you must not speak." Borrowing a metaphor used by C. S. Lewis in another context, our particular traditions are like the different rooms of a great house, and the public square is like the entrance parlor. The parlor is indispensable; it is where everyone meets and goes in and out. But we learn even our parlor manners in the family rooms, the family rooms are where people actually live, and one of the chief topics of parlor conversation is—surprise! —our families.

To be sure, members of different traditions cannot always speak together, but sometimes they can, and in ways that traditionless people never can. Although I am not an orthodox Jew, I see and respect what an orthodox Jew is getting at; a rootless modern has no idea. It was no accident that the period during which the thinkers of my faith achieved their greatest insights into natural law coincided with the period during which they were intensely and simultaneously engaged with the pagan thought of Aristotle, the Jewish thought of Maimonides, and the Muslim thought of Averroës. A Jewish thinker who is writing about the natural law will naturally draw from the resources of Judaism to do so; he will give far more attention than I do to the rabbinical tradition of reflection upon the "reasons of the laws" and to the ancient Jewish idea of a Noahide covenant which precedes the Abrahamic and Mosaic. Nevertheless, I too can reflect on these with profit, for they have leavened my tradition already.

The greater difficulty lies in speaking with people who have *no* traditions of unfolding the natural law, only "traditions" of evading it. Although this kind of conversation is not impossible, it presents special difficulties which are best reserved for a later point in our discussion. We can better teach speech to the mute if we have learned it among people who speak.

What It Is That We Can't Not Know

*A restatement of what the natural law tradition
has always thought to be "written on the heart."*

C OOPER CONCLUDED that the universal moral code "agrees rather
closely with our own Decalogue taken in a strictly literal sense."
There is another way to think of this: that the biblical Decalogue, or Ten Commandments, states the most important part of the
universal moral code in ideal form. If the anthropological data suggest
something short of the ideal, that is not because nothing is universal,
but because two universals are in conflict: universal moral knowledge
and universal desire to evade it. The first one we owe to our creation.
The second we owe to our fall.

This is how the Christian branch of the natural law tradition has
viewed the Decalogue. The great natural lawyer Thomas Aquinas is
quite clear about it. His admirers often ask "Why don't he and the other
natural law thinkers say what the natural laws *are?*" I have heard the
question asked by distinguished scholars. But he does; if they would read
a little further, they would see that he thinks they are well summarized
by the Ten Commandments.[1] We misread him because of our own secular prejudice that natural law and biblical revelation are completely

unrelated. His view is that, having both come from the same Lawmaker, they illuminate each other.

The Decalogue is not an exhaustive summary, but a suggestive summary. It does not include all of our natural moral knowledge, but it either states, implies, or presupposes a good deal of it. For example, the First Commandment states that only God is to be worshipped as God, but it presupposes the knowledge of God as well as several principles of justice, including the principle of gratitude and the principle "Give to each what is due to him." The Sixth Commandment states merely that adultery is wrong, but it presupposes the institution of matrimony, and implies that there is something special about it, thereby suggesting a much broader norm of sexual purity. The Eighth Commandment states merely that one must not bear false witness, but it presupposes provisions for public justice, and suggests that we should seek to extend the truthfulness of relationships in general. To elucidate every implication and presupposition of the Decalogue would take more than a chapter, indeed more than a set of books. For this reason our own discussion must be written in such broad strokes that one could read while running.

THE CLASSICAL ENUMERATION

We will consider each of the Ten Commandments in turn, then consider them as a set.[2] First come several Commandments about what is owed to God; then a larger number about what is owed to neighbor. To some it seems odd that duties to God should be reckoned part of the *natural* law, because they obviously presuppose some sort of faith. Up to a point, the natural law tradition agrees. For example, although Thomas Aquinas says that all ten of the Commandments are in some sense self-evident, he makes a distinction between those which are evident to every mind and those which are evident to the faithful mind.[3] It may seem as though he is contradicting himself: if some of them require faith, doesn't that mean they are *not* evident?

But there is no contradiction. Faith readjusts disordered mental powers so that we can *recognize* that the evident is evident—something like removing our fingers from our ears so that the music we have been listening to sounds more like what it is. In truth, every created intellect hears the music of its Creator. As Paul puts it, "Ever since the creation of the world His invisible nature, namely, His eternal power and deity, has been clearly perceived in the things that have been made."[4] The difficulty is that we human beings are prone to neglect even our duties to neighbors whom we can see; how much more prone are we to neglect our duties to God whom we cannot see. We are tempted to lavish the *sensus divinitatis* on things that are not divine. Faith—"the conviction of things not seen" (Hebrews 11:1, RSV)—is the virtue which enables us to resist this temptation. It is a kind of confidence, not "blind" in the sense of being unjustified, but justified by other means than sight. God is not the only thing of which we have conviction without sight. We cannot see our minds, our purposes, or our sensory experiences; some philosophers of mind refuse to believe in these things either. Yet we have good reason to believe that they are real.

These reflections help to understand why Thomas connected self-evidence with faith. Faith—the right kind of faith—turns out to be not only a spiritual but an intellectual virtue, and the failure to acknowledge God is not a gap in our natural knowledge, but a failure to keep troth with it. The Commandments concerning God belong to the natural law just as surely as the ones concerning our neighbor do. Let us turn now to the First Commandment.

1   *I am the* Lord *your God, who brought you out of the land of Egypt, out of the house of bondage. You shall have no other gods before me. You shall not make for yourself a graven image, or any likeness of anything that is in heaven above, or that is on the earth beneath, or that is in the water under the earth; you shall not bow down to them or serve them; for I the* Lord *your God am a jealous God, visiting*

*the iniquity of the fathers upon the children to the third and fourth
generation of those who hate me, but showing steadfast love to thousands of those who love me and keep my commandments*
(Deuteronomy 5, vv. 6-10).

The point of the First Commandment is that the one true God,
and only the one true God, is to be worshipped as God. To hold that
this biblical injunction belongs equally to the *natural* law is to hold that
although not everyone believes the Bible as the word of God, everyone
does know that there is one true God and that he owes Him sole worship. If this is true, then those who say they don't know of any such God
are fooling themselves, and biblical revelation merely "blows their cover."

The Commandment presupposes more than just the knowledge that
God is real. It presupposes that we also understand that benefit incurs
obligation, supreme benefit incurs supreme obligation, and we are indebted to God for benefits beyond all others. This in turn presupposes
that we know the principle, "Give to each what is due to him," what we
owe God being loyalty, worship, and obedience. To deny Him is the
deepest form of treason—much more serious than the ordinary sort.

The Commandment does not presuppose that God needs our de-
votion—only that we owe it to Him. If it is asked why He requires what
He does not need, the answer is found in the nature He has imparted
to us. As rational and moral beings, we are endowed with the capacity
to recognize what is intrinsically worthy of our gratitude. To pay this
kind of debt ennobles us rather than demeaning us; to withhold it is a
distortion of rational nature which puts us lower than the beasts.

Just what supreme boon does incur our obligation to God may be
unclear. Not all people are indebted to God for release from the land of
Egypt; that grace was for the Hebrews. But the natural law tradition
has pointed out that all people are indebted to God for their being, and
held that at some level we all know it. Friedrich Nietzsche, originator
of the slogan "God is dead," reported that at times he was overcome by

gratitude. This admission is most interesting, because gratitude is not a self-regarding attitude like pleasure, but an other-regarding attitude like anger. It presupposes someone to whom gratitude is owed.

It is interesting that the Hebrews should have been reminded of a particular rather than a universal benefit. Such is our fallen condition that we are not impressed by the stupendous boon of creation; always we are asking God "What have you done for me *lately*?" Christianity returns to the theme of His recent benefits, holding that He offers release from another land of Egypt—the deeper house of bondage of which Egypt is the image, the burden of the fall itself. But these things go beyond the natural law.

2   *You shall not take the name of the* LORD *your God in vain: for the* LORD *will not hold him guiltless who takes his name in vain* (v.11).

A paraphrase of the Second Commandment might be "You shall not use empty speech in connection with God." The specific application is to the empty use of His name—to the word which *means* Him—but by implication it forbids every form of light, careless, dishonest, contemptuous, hypocritical, or blasphemous speech about Him.

To say that this is one of the things we can't not know—that it belongs not only to biblical injunction but to natural law—is to say that we naturally understand certain things about the relation of speech to reality, a theme to which we return in Commandment Eight. Even a liar's speech expresses something true; it may not tell us the state of the world, but it tells us the state of his heart. What empty God-talk tells us is that where there ought to be God, there is emptiness.

3   *Observe the sabbath day, to keep it holy, as the* LORD *your God commanded you. Six days you shall labor, and do all your work; but the seventh day is a sabbath to the* LORD *your God; in it you shall not*

do any work, you, or your son, or your daughter, or your manser-
vant, or your maidservant, or your ox, or your ass, or any of your
cattle, or the sojourner who is within your gates, that your manser-
vant and your maidservant may rest as well as you. You shall re-
member that you were a servant in the land of Egypt, and the LORD
your God brought you out thence with a mighty hand and an out-
stretched arm; therefore the LORD *your God commanded you to keep*
the sabbath day (vv.12-14).[5]

The Third Commandment declares that complete engrossment in mundane affairs is not merely tiring but debasing; one of the principles of our design is that times be set apart just for the remembrance of God. A presupposition of the Commandment is that although the created world in which we go about our labors is real and important, the Creator is more important still. Also presupposed is that we are built to run in cycles. It isn't possible for beings of our kind to do everything all the time; we need to do some things sometimes and other things at other times. Thus someone who says "My work is my worship" is deceiving himself—or else worshipping his work. Yes, we should do all our labors as though for God; but for God, we should intermit our labors.

Traditionally, these presuppositions of the biblical injunction have been regarded as belonging to the natural law. Of course the biblical injunction goes further, requiring that labor and intermission come in cycles of precisely seven days. This has *not* been regarded as belonging to the natural law.[6] As in several other Commandments, the universal and particular are mixed.

4 *Honor your father and your mother, as the* LORD *your God com-*
    manded you; that your days may be prolonged, and that it may go
    well with you, in the land which the LORD *your God gives you* (v.16).

The point of the Fourth Commandment is that parents are God's delegated representatives to their children. To dishonor their authority dishonors the one who appoints them. In the biblical injunction they are appointed expressly, by words. According to the natural law tradition, they are also appointed tacitly, by the inclination to procreation and care of family which the Creator has imparted to us.

Scholars of the family have slowly, against great ideological pressure, been rediscovering this feature of our design. As two sociologists observe, "If we were asked to design a system for making sure that children's basic needs were met, we would probably come up with something quite similar to the two-parent ideal. Such a design, in theory, would not only ensure that children had access to the time and money of two adults, it also would provide a system of checks and balances that promoted quality parenting. The fact that both parents have a biological connection to the child would increase the likelihood that the parents would identify with the child and be willing to sacrifice for that child, and it would reduce the likelihood that either parent would abuse the child."[7]

5　*You shall not kill* (v.17).

Our translations of the Fifth Commandment are somewhat misleading, in that the primary meaning of the Hebrew verb rendered "kill" is "murder."[8] Not all killing is murder, and the injunction has not traditionally been taken to forbid self-defense, capital punishment, or just war. So seriously did Hebrew law take bloodshed, however, that even justified wartime killing was thought to bring about ritual impurity. The biblical ground of the prohibition of murder is that man is the created image of God: "Whoever sheds the blood of man, by man shall his blood be shed; for God made man in his own image" (Genesis 9:6). In biblical terms, to say that man is God's created image is to say that the eternal God made man such a being that it was possible for God to have communion with him. It also means that he is God's representative on earth, with a steward's authority over the rest of creation.

How much of this carries over into natural law? It is certainly one of the things we can't not know that no one may deliberately take innocent human life. The more particular doctrine of man as the created image of God seems unknown beyond the bible's sphere of influence; it is not one of the things we can't not know. Some intuition of the sacredness of human life is universal nonetheless, and this foothold in our nature is what makes the doctrine of the *imago Dei* so compelling once heard. In this sense it might be said that nature contains a premonition of biblical revelation. Unfortunately, the intuition of the sacredness of human life can easily be deflected into various forms of idolatry, in which we reverence *ourselves*—as God, partly-God, parts *of* God, gods, or on the way to becoming gods.

Insofar as this deflection requires exaggerating one of the things we can't not know (that human life is sacred) while suppressing another (that humans are not divine), it is profoundly dishonest. That does not prevent it from being common, and the same two-edged potentiality for good or evil, for development or perversion, can be found in every natural intuition.

6   *Neither shall you commit adultery.* (v.18.)

In the biblical context, the Sixth Commandment is but one of many regulations regarding the sexual powers—but it is the most important. Its specific point is to forbid any married person from having sexual relations with anyone but his spouse. Except on the supposition that there is such a thing as marriage—a lasting covenant between one man and one woman for a procreative union of complements—it makes no sense. But the supposition is justified. Marriage is a universal institution, and the potentiality for it, like the potentiality for family, is built into human nature.

Not only does every culture recognize marriage, but everywhere it is esteemed above other erotic relationships. Even where concubinage is tolerated, a concubine does not have the status of a wife; even where casual liaisons are tolerated, a pickup does not have the status of a concubine. Although exceptions are known, they have been short-lived. For example, the medieval practice of "courtly" love temporarily held the relationship of knight and lady higher than the relationship of husband and wife—but the most interesting thing about the practice is that whatever had value in it was eventually absorbed into our matrimonial traditions, and whatever could not be absorbed into our matrimonial traditions died out.

A striking feature of marriage is that it is always bilateral: *one* man, *one* woman. This feature may be blurred by the fact that in some places a man is permitted to have several wives; even then, however, he is understood to have entered into several marriages, not one marriage to several women. Moreover, although polygamy and polyandry are both sometimes tolerated, they are nowhere tolerated both at once: The situation in which Fred is married to Beth and Amy, Beth to Fred and Tom, Tom to Beth and Frieda, and Frieda to Tom and Sam, is not found anywhere. Another striking feature of marriage is that it is always one *man* and one *woman*. This is not hard to understand either. In the first place, a man and man (or woman and woman) are not complements, but sames; when their relationship is sexualized, rather than balancing each other they drive each other to extremes. In the second place, both sexes are needed for procreation—and not just because a man cannot make another man pregnant. Both sexes are needed to raise the child, because the female is better designed for nurture and the male for protection and discipline; both are needed to teach the child, because every young one needs a model of his own sex as well as the other. Children need a Mom and a Dad, not a Mom and Mom or a Dad and Dad.

Is there a best form of marriage? The trend in countries which once tolerated polygamy has been to ban it. On the other hand, for most of history the monogamous West has been somewhat out of step with the rest of the human race. Even in the West, moreover, although the ethical ideal has been absolute monogamy, the legal norm has been merely relative monogamy, which is also known as successive polygamy. What is one to make of this? Among natural law thinkers, the traditional view is that the superiority of monogamy is *not* one of the things we can't not know—but that it is plain upon reflection. Simultaneous polygamy reflects and reinforces a rigid hierarchy among men in which the number of one's wives is an index of prestige. By producing a shortage of marriageable females, it causes hardship among males who do not belong to the privileged strata. Polygamy, whether of the simultaneous or successive sort, undermines spousal intimacy, weakens the bond between father and child, turns women into social inferiors (or at least increases their vulnerability), and kindles jealousy—not only among different wives, but among the children of different wives.

Besides, polygamy cannot satisfy the heart. Aren't love poems all over the world addressed from the Lover to the Beloved? A lyric "to my darlings, Mary, Ellen, Susan, Penelope, Martha, Hortense, and Gwen" would be recognized everywhere as farce.

7   *Neither shall you steal.* (v.19.)

As the Fourth Commandment presupposes the institution of the family and the Sixth Commandment presupposes the institution of marriage, so the Seventh Commandment presupposes the institution of personal property. The point of the Commandment is that no one shall take from another what belongs to him against his reasonable will. Natural law tradition has claimed that this precept too is universally known. To be sure, there is a good deal of disagreement among the peoples of the world as to what kinds of things may become personal property, how much personal property may be accumulated, and what limits there should be on its use. Such questions belong to the remoter parts of the natural law, not its first principles. Nevertheless, all recognize such a thing as personal property, all recognize that theft is wrong—and socialists do not like having their pockets picked any better than capitalists do.

Even arguments against the Seventh Commandment pay it homage between the lines. Take for example the argument that it cannot be wrong for a starving man to steal a bit of food from one who has plenty but refuses to part with it. Those who propose this line of reasoning may think they are disputing the Seventh Commandment, but they are really disputing only a common misunderstanding of it: That no one may take from another against his *will*. They stand *with* the Commandment as it is rightly understood: That no one may take from another what belongs to him against his *reasonable* will. The will may be unreasonable; for example, it is unreasonable for the owner to withhold what he has in plenty at the cost of his neighbor's life. The point here is not that some thefts are permitted, but that some takings should not be considered thefts.

The "reasonableness" proviso is not something tacked on by overly clever natural lawyers. It merely spells out the plain sense of common people—the only possible warrant for saying that it does belong to the basics of natural law. The biblical code acknowledges the same point, driving it home in a variety of ways. For example, not only were Hebrew farmers required to allow the poor to glean what they could from the harvested fields, but they were also required to make sure that there was something left for the poor to glean. The corners of the field were not to be harvested at all.

Needless to say, if theft is taking from another against his reasonable will, then there may arise cases where it is difficult to tell what is reasonable, and we will sometimes get them wrong. The natural law tradition does not deny this. Its claim is merely that everyone grasps the point of the Seventh Commandment—not that everyone applies it without error. Some are wiser at such things than others.

Another difficulty is that any point which does require interpretation opens up the possibility of making excuses. Psychologist David T. Lykken tells of a fifteen-year-old who stole a car at gunpoint. Later the boy rationalized his actions by asking, "How else was I s'posed to get home, man?" He was claiming that it would have been *unreasonable* to expect him to wait an hour for the next bus, and therefore that he was innocent of wrong.[9] Although people who concoct such justifications are often said to lack conscience, the sheer fact that the boy *could* concoct the justification shows that he knew how the Seventh Commandment works. Some people lack guilty feelings—but nobody lacks basic moral knowledge.[10]

8   *Neither shall you bear false witness against your neighbor* (v.20).

The Eighth Commandment is often misunderstood. Bearing false witness isn't lying *per se,* but lying to get someone in trouble—especially in a judicial context, where one is offering evidence. A presupposition of the Eighth Commandment, then, is that some sort of provision has been made for public justice. No people in the world lives without some such customs. The chieftain of the smallest tribe is expected to hear disputes and judge justly. Like marriage and family, the office of judge would seem to be a spontaneous and natural human institution. The fundamental act of government is not legislation, but judgment.

Whether lying *per se* is wrong—whether it is always wrong to say, with the intent to deceive, what is contrary to what I understand to be the truth—is another question.[11] Natural law thinkers have always conceded that this is a genuinely difficult problem, the solution to which is plainly *not* among the things we can't not know. I must not lie to achieve injustice; that much is plain. But may I lie to prevent it? Because of the difficulty of this issue we need to spend more time on the Eighth Commandment than on the others.

The classical illustration of the quandary is whether I may tell a would-be murderer who is looking for a man that I am hiding, "I have no information as to his whereabouts." Some natural law thinkers have said that I may never lie, period; to the would-be murderer at the door, I should reply "You have no right to ask such a question, and I will not answer it." Let's call that Opinion One. Of course such an answer exposes me to danger, but that cannot be helped; justice is never safe. The greater difficulty is that it exposes the hiding man to danger, and I have promised him my protection. Is that right? Other natural law thinkers have said that it is *not* right; they argue that I may lie just when the questioner has no right to the truth that he demands—as in the case of the would-be murderer, because he desires it solely for the purpose of committing injustice. Let's call that Opinion Two. Still other natural law thinkers have said that although I should *never* lie, I may equivocate. For example, the sentence "I have no information" is an equivocation if I say it with the meaning, "I have no information *for you.*" Let's call that Opinion Three.

Opinion Three may seem rather sticky, but it does have a certain plausibility. After all, the meaning of words depends on shared understandings. It might be argued that when the receptionist tells callers "The boss is not in," she is not lying because *everyone knows* that not every caller has the right to know the whereabouts of the boss, and because, in our culture, one of the possible meanings of receptionist's statement is "The boss is not in *to take calls.*" She does not intend to deceive, and no one is actually deceived.

Now in the case of the receptionist the shared understanding arises from convention—she and the caller follow the same telephoning customs. What about the case of the murderer at my door? If there is a shared understanding in that case, it would have to arise from the natural law—because the murderer knows the basic moral rules as well as I do. One of the things that he and I both know is that nobody has a moral right to an answer to a question which he has no moral right to ask, and another of the things that he and I both know is that we normally take this fact into account in interpreting the responses which people *do* give to illicit questions.

In other words, the murderer at the door knows as well as anyone else that the response to an illicit question is normally equivocal. This would seem to make his question pointless. Yet he asks it anyway—as though he had forgotten that it were illicit. Perhaps in a sense he *has* forgotten. For most people, murder is difficult, precisely because they know that it is wrong. Consequently, a man planning murder may try not to think about the evil of his intended act. So what? If he is trying not to think about the evil of the act, then he is probably trying not to think about the evil of his question either. The upshot is that the more guilty his conscience, the more naïve his expectations; an equivocal answer may catch him by surprise. There is certainly a deception—but perhaps he deceives himself.

One striking fact is that the advocates of Opinion Two and Opinion Three seem to be approving and disapproving exactly the same statements. They differ only about whether to call them lies. The former say *"You may lie* just when the other party has no right to the truth he demands"; the latter say "You may never lie, but *you may equivocate* just when the other party has no right to the truth he demands." To put the matter another way, the latter do not consider every lie in the literal sense as a lie in the moral sense.

Of course there is a risk in allowing people to get out of corners by equivocating. They may concoct private definitions like "it is" for "it isn't," "I promise" for "I don't promise," and "I'm not married" for "I'm married"—just to have an excuse for treating statements which are not at all equivocal as though they were. In American politics the paramount example of private definition comes from former president Bill Clinton, who justified a perjury in an impeachment deposition with the explanation "It all depends on what 'is' is." Another problem is that even if we agree with the advocates of Opinion Three that equivocations do not share in the intrinsic badness of lies, they certainly tend to share in at least one bad result of lies: When people are on the receiving end of an equivocation, they may feel tricked, so that the trust and confidence necessary to hearty social life are diminished.

To eliminate the first risk and ameliorate the second, the advocates of Opinion Three insist on certain restrictions: (1) Private definitions are illicit; no equivocation which relies on them can ever be justified; (2) even the honest sort of equivocation should be avoided unless the risk of evil is grave; and (3) anyone who has a right to the truth has a right to receive it straight; in this case equivocation is flatly forbidden. Moreover, (4) when a justified equivocation fails to hold off a threatened evil, even then an outright lie is wrong. It is better to suffer wrong than to do it. Some will call these cautions and distinctions "splitting hairs." Why not say, "When telling the truth would produce injustice, go ahead and lie?" Perhaps because our uneasiness about lying runs deeper than the bad consequences that lying usually produces; we sense that lying is somehow wrong *in itself,* that words are ordained for truth. This is why we are so uncomfortable when people try to finesse the problem of the murderer at the door by saying that "the end justifies the means." It is too much like saying "wrong is not wrong," or "what must not be done may be done." A wiser counsel is that we must not do evil that good may result. The disagreement between the advocates of Opinion One and advocates of Opinions Two and Three concerns how best to honor this counsel.

9   *Neither shall you covet your neighbor's wife* (v.21a).

Nominally the Ninth Commandment addresses only the husband— neither shall you covet your neighbor's *wife*—but it has always been taken as addressing both spouses, in the same way that the word "man," in English, can refer to people of both sexes.

The point of the Ninth Commandment is to heighten the Sixth Commandment. Both concern the respect which is due to one's neighbor in the integrity of his family, but the Sixth regulates the outward life of our limbs, while the Ninth regulates the inward life of our desires. What's wrong with sexual desire? Nothing is wrong with it *per se*; the problem lies not in sexual desire but in misdirected sexual desire. And this problem is very great. Keeping my hands off my neighbor's wife is so important that I shouldn't even wish to put my hands on her.

Our own popular culture denies that we are responsible for our desires. "I can't help it that I feel that way; I just do." It's true that we can't simply shut off unwanted longings, and it's also true that the very effort of suppressing them stirs them up. Even so, our control over our inward life is much greater than we like to admit. Although I may not be able to keep an unwanted guest from entering the house of my thoughts, or to force her outside after she has entered them, yet nothing forces me to ask her in. Nor am I compelled to sit down and admire her, to enjoy her attentions, or to invite her to play with my imagination. If I ignore her and go on about my business, she will eventually leave my mind on her own; if I pet her, say "Don't go yet," and tell her what a lovely thought she is, she will return another day in power, and that day she will burn down the house. Viewed this way, covetousness is bad not only because it leads to adultery, but in itself.

We have not all followed this path to the bitter end, but we do all know how indulgence affects the imagination. That is why the Ninth Commandment is a part of the natural law. To the pop culture mantra "I can't help my feelings," it replies "You know better."

   10   *And you shall not desire your neighbor's house, his field, or his man-servant, or his maidservant, his ox, or his ass, or anything that is your neighbor's* (v.21b).

As the Ninth Commandment heightens the Sixth Commandment, so the Tenth Commandment heightens the Seventh. The difference is that the Ninth concerns the respect due to neighbor in the integrity of his family, while the Tenth concerns the respect due to him in the integrity of his belongings. It is good that I do not steal his property, but that is not enough. I must not desire it in the first place; I must not entertain the thought "If only it were mine instead of his." The rich should not covet the ox of the poor, nor the poor the ass of the rich.

Nor, for that matter, should the middle-class interest group covet the benefits which accrue to the other interest groups. It is difficult to conceive how profoundly our politics, economics, and everyday life would change if the Tenth Commandment were taken seriously. Hardly anyone does take it seriously, but that is quite different from saying that hardly anyone knows it to be true. We all know that it is wrong to be a thief; it would be pretty difficult to know this and yet *not* know that it is wrong to have thievish desires.

The presupposition of both the Ninth and Tenth Commandments is that the right ordering of life depends on more than the mere performance and avoidance of various outward deeds. It takes in the entire inward life. This presupposition can be applied to all ten of the Commandments. Idols must be abolished, not only from your hearth, but from your heart. It is just as wicked to think empty thoughts of God as to speak them. Keep the day of reverence, not with your body only, but with your whole being. Serve your parents not only with your lips, but with your spirit. Foreswear not only murder, but even malicious thoughts. Not only must you abandon the use of lies to ensnare your neighbor, but you must not even desire that he be ensnared.

IS THERE A PATTERN?

Many thinkers believe that everyday moral rules like the ones we have been discussing are really just offscourings of some Deeper Consideration. The idea is that if you know the Deeper Consideration, you can derive all the moral rules. In my introduction I commented briefly on utilitarianism, the most popular form of this doctrine. According to utilitarians, the Deeper Consideration is pleasure, and maximizing it is the only absolute. If you think of the world as an enormous cistern, with pleasures pouring into it, pains draining out of it, and all the dogs and rats and humans just so many drains and faucets, then you see the world as the utilitarian sees it. It doesn't matter what happens to the individual faucets; what matters is the level in the tank. From this point of view, if rules like "Do not murder" have any value at all, it isn't because they are right in themselves, but because they tend to increase the net pleasure.

I leave aside the peculiarity of viewing ourselves as drains and faucets. The greater problem is this. If increasing net pleasure is the only reason for following the everyday moral rules, and if we can think of a better way to increase net pleasure, then we don't have to follow the rules. Consider, for example, the hanging of innocent persons. The utilitarian agrees that it is not a good idea—generally speaking. In the first place, the anticipation of being hanged makes people unhappy. In the second place, by hanging people we lose the pleasure they might have experienced had they lived, not to mention their contribution to the happiness of others. But wait—the coin has another side. Maybe some of these persons are unhappy anyway. Besides, holding trials to ascertain guilt and innocence is tedious and costly, and that reduces pleasure too. Why not give up holding trials? It might be possible to achieve at least one of the happy results of doing justice—deterring crime—by convincing people that justice has been done without actually doing it. Suppose that instead of holding trials, we periodically selected a certain number of persons at random, then executed them—merely taking care to tell the public afterward that they had been tried and found guilty. Quite possibly, a greater balance of pleasure over pain would accrue from the new method than from the old one. If so, the utilitarian would have to say "Go to it." So much for the Fifth and Eighth Commandments.

"Rule" utilitarians have an answer to this criticism: Don't decide which *acts* to commit by weighing the effect of various *acts* on the level in the cistern; instead, decide which *rules* to follow by weighing the effect of following various *rules* on the level in the cistern. Suppose we agree to this procedure. Then which rule about murder shall we adopt? From a utilitarian point of view, "Never kill an innocent person" would seem an unlikely candidate; there are too many cases in which the innocent fellow is unpopular and others would be happier to see him die. How about "Never kill an innocent person *unless most people would rather see him dead*"? Or "Never kill an innocent person *unless most people think that he is guilty*"? Perhaps "Never mind guilt or innocence—*kill everyone who makes no contribution to society*"? It seems that the Fifth Commandment is doomed even if we do become "rule" utilitarians. Given a choice between discarding the Fifth Commandment and discarding the utilitarian theory, conscience bids us do the latter.

The natural law tradition denies all such theories which view the everyday moral rules as merely instruments for advancing some Deeper Consideration. From the natural law perspective, the patterns of conduct marked out by the Commandments are not only right, but right *in themselves*. If this is true, two things follow. First, we are not permitted to transgress them for the sake of supposedly "greater" ends, like telling lies to elect good men to office. Second, we are not permitted to trade them off against each other, like committing a few more murders to achieve a larger reduction in thefts. The technical terms for these two qualities of the Commandments are "inviolable" and "nonsubstitutable."

That the basic moral laws are inviolable and nonsubstitutable does not mean that we cannot summarize them; we do not have to recite them all every time we wish to speak of them. The mere fact that they cannot be derived from some Deeper Consideration does not mean that they have no pattern. It only means that *that* is not their pattern.

As a matter of fact, a great many more or less satisfactory summaries have been proposed. Perhaps the simplest formula was suggested by Thomas Aquinas: "Good is to be done and pursued, and evil is to be avoided." Now there is no greater natural law thinker in all of history than Thomas, but his formula does have a serious drawback. It invites a misunderstanding—a catastrophic misunderstanding—which makes it *seem* to resemble the utilitarian philosophy. In our day, most people who hear a statement like "Good is to be done" take it to mean that right behavior is merely a strategy for achieving some undifferentiated "stuff," called "good," which functions in the same way that pleasure functions in the utilitarian calculations. The actual view of Thomas Aquinas could hardly be more different. Good in his view is richly differentiated. The various goods differ from one another even more than the primary colors do, and they cannot fill in for each other. The only reason Thomas uses the abstract term "good" at all is to remind us that despite their utterly irreducible differences, the various goods do have this in common—*that they are good.* By the design of Creation, they attract. We are drawn to them by more than our desires; we are moved to them as to ends. The problem with the Thomistic formula is not that it is wrong, but that it sounds as though it meant something else.

Another disadvantage of the Thomistic formula is that it gives the impression that the two kinds of goods that we serve—the good which we serve in God, and the goods which we serve in neighbor—are merely two different species of the same broader genus, "good." The fact—and this staggers and awes the heart—the fact is that the good which we serve in God is good in a different *sense* than the goods which we serve in neighbor, and the two do not belong on the same plane at all. Here is how it is. The only categories we even have for conceiving of goodness are the categories provided to us in Creation—in the order of the created world around us, and the answering order of our created intellects. But God's goodness is the unimaginable *uncreated* goodness which is capable of contriving *for* us these categories. We cannot conceive of the uncreated Good as He is in Himself; we can only speak of Him by analogy with the created possibilities of goodness into which He has poured us. For example we compare him with coolness and drink: "As a hart longs for flowing streams, so longs my soul for thee, O God." Although Thomas himself is one of the greatest expositors of this teaching, his formula does not measure up to his insight. Rightly understood, it isn't *wrong;* the problem, as before, it that it is hardly ever rightly understood.

Later on, where Thomas is speaking more particularly of the Decalogue, he offers a second summary, this one drawn directly from the Bible. This second summary—which can be recognized as superior even apart from considerations of divine revelation—is more complex than his first one. It also proceeds differently, summarizing the basic moral laws not primarily in terms of an abstract good, but in terms of a personal relationship. From the Bible itself:

> *You shall love the* LORD *your God with all your heart, and with all your soul, and with all your mind. This is the first and great commandment. And a second is like it, You shall love your neighbor as yourself. On these two commandments depend all the law and the prophets.*[12]

Traditionally called simply the Summary of the Law, this biblical synopsis is plainly twofold: it includes one precept to love God and another precept to love my neighbor as myself (for he is, like myself, His created image). The latter precept is sometimes given in the equivalent form, traditionally called the Golden Rule, which runs "And as you wish that men would do to you, do so to them."[13] Equally plainly the Summary presupposes that I love myself, but it does not command me to do so. There is no need, because everyone loves himself already. Even the suicide desires his own good: he wrongly imagines that he would be better off dead. The moral problem is not that we love ourselves but that we love ourselves the wrong way.

As Thomas explains, these two precepts to love God and neighbor "are the first general principles of the natural law, and are self-evident to human reason."[14] Both precepts are inviolable, neither is substitutable, and in this sense, neither has priority. But in another sense the former does have priority—it is more grave, more important, as the root is more important than the branch.[15] Another difference is that the love of God, as commanded by the former precept, should be beyond measure, while the love of neighbor, as commanded by the latter precept, should be proportioned to the proper love of self. To be sure, this is a very high proportion. If I really loved my neighbor as myself I would die for him. But the love of God should exceed even that. Justice alone might teach us so much, were we only able to gaze steadily upon it— for if God is truly God, then in the most literal of senses one we owe everything to Him. Render unto each his due.

In the context of the Decalogue, the love of God is spelled out in Commandments One through Four (some say One through Three), sometimes called the First Tablet; the love of neighbor is spelled out in the rest of the Commandments, sometimes called the Second Tablet. The nature of this "spelling out" is crucial. It is not that the Decalogue is *deduced* from the Summary of the Law. Rather, it is in the light of the more particular Commandments that we first understand what loving God and neighbor means.[16] For how am I to do unto men as I would wish that they do to me, unless I first know what I should wish? Eventually the relationship comes to work in the other direction too: once we recognize what love it is that the more particular commandments spell out, we come to understand them more deeply than we did at first.

Something else happens as well. By continually feeding upon these basic expressions of the natural law—the Decalogue and the Summary— the mind also gains more strength in recognizing their remote implications. How this happens is not fully understood. It is not that one becomes more skilled in logical deduction, but that one gradually gains clearer insight.

If we admit that the Decalogue belongs not only to revealed but to natural law, then we must admit that the Summary belongs to it too.

Yes, they appear in the Bible; yes, the Bible illuminates them; but the knowledge of them is anterior to the Bible, and they can be recognized as true apart from it. To readers of my own faith I add that this does not make the Bible dispensable. It explains why the Bible is believable.

— 3 —

Could We Get By Knowing Less?

*Whether we could know what we owe to our neighbor
even without knowing that we owe anything to God.*

ALTHOUGH I HAVE EMPHASIZED that the reality of God and our in-
debtedness to Him are among the things everyone really knows,
I have also remarked how scandalous some people find this
claim. They deny the natural knowledge of God, of the First Tablet of
the Decalogue, and of the Summary of the Law, and they would prefer
to acknowledge neighbor only. Passions run high among such thinkers.
A reviewer of one of my earlier books angrily declared that "God does
not belong in political theory." Because he agreed that politics has a
moral foundation, I suppose he thought God did not belong in ethics
either. A scholar of my acquaintance has devoted the last phase of his
intellectual career to what he calls "pushing God out of the natural
law"—or at least, he says, "into the wings." This is a widely shared goal.
Insofar as it wishes to get by on the Second Tablet without the First,
we might call it the Second Tablet Project.

The Second Tablet Project is probably more popular among luke-
warm religious believers who wish to make the moral law palatable to
nonbelievers than it is among nonbelievers themselves. Nonbelievers

who want to get rid of the First Tablet usually have doubts about the
Second too. And for the same reasons. God is a dubious proposition,
they reflect; but why should morality be less dubious than He? In their
view, these two matters are both pretty dim. As to the notion of "things
we can't not know," they think there aren't any—just a lot of incompatible opinions about God and how to live, all of them equally controversial, because none of them can be known to be true. Under the
circumstances, they think, the only sensible thing to do is to eject the
whole lot of these opinions from the public square. This is the mental-
ity that finds it scandalous to post the Ten Commandments on a court-
room wall. The argument seems to be "Because we don't agree with each
other, you must do as I say"—for, if anyone should protest "But your
opinion is just as controversial as the ones you complain about," they
respond "See what I mean?" Or perhaps, like John Rawls, they respond
that *their* opinion should have special privileges because it is "political,
not metaphysical."[1] Here the argument seems to be "The ultimate truth
of things is unknowable, and *that's* why you must do as I say." Of course,
any view of what is knowable or unknowable presupposes something
about ultimate truth, so that too is sleight of hand.

The fact that the Second Tablet Project so often turns into a No
Tablet project raises an important question. What difference does it make
to the knowledge of the moral law that we *do* have some knowledge of
God? If we didn't have that knowledge, *could* we retain knowledge of
the moral law? If we could retain it, would it be different?

The inquiry has two parts, because there are two ways to know about
God: the vague, partial, natural knowledge of God which is available to
every human being, and the additional knowledge of God which is
offered (for those who accept it) in the biblical tradition of direct revelation. Though my emphasis is on the first way, I will comment on the
second too. To be sure, the Bible is not included in the things one can't
not know. But every perspective for discussing what we can't not know
is *some* perspective, and my perspective is biblical.

By the first way to know about God I mean the spontaneous aware-ness of the reality of the Creator. I do not exclude the clarity that phi-losophy can add to this awareness; I only wish to point out that the philosophical arguments for the existence of God do not start from nowhere. However complex they may be, they merely elaborate *pre-*philosophical intuitions, such as the everyday idea that anything which does not *have to be* requires a cause. "Why is there something, rather than nothing?" is a question that anyone can ask.

As to the second way of knowing about God—the biblical tradi-tion of direct revelation—I use the qualifier "biblical" advisedly. Other religions have traditions too, but traditions of direct revelation are quite rare. Every major religion which claims to record God's direct revela-tions to human beings in actual historical time accepts at least part of the Bible; this includes Judaism, Christianity, and Islam. No major re-ligion outside of the biblical orbit does claim to record God's direct revelations to human beings in actual historical time.

THE FIRST PART OF THE INQUIRY

Apart from any consideration of an alleged direct revelation, what difference does it make to the natural law that we *naturally* have knowl-edge of God?

The abolition of man. If God has designed and endowed us with our nature—this is not a question of how He did it or how long it took, only of who is responsible—then we can be confident that we have the nature that we ought to have in accord with His good purposes.[2] Let us imagine someone who denies the premise. He admits that human beings have a nature, in the sense that certain ways of living go against the grain; he only refuses to allow that we were endowed with this na-ture by God. We are to regard the direction of the grain as the result of a meaningless and purposeless process that did not have us in mind.[3]

I think it follows that had the process gone a bit differently—had our ancestors been carnivores instead of omnivores, had they laid eggs instead of borne live young, or had they never left the oceans for the land—then we would have had a different nature. Given the nature that we do have, certain things go against the grain, hence the natural law. Honor your father and mother. Do not kill. Do not covet. Given some other nature, other things would have gone against the grain—hence some *other* natural law. It might have been anything. Supplant your father. Chase away your mother. Eat your neighbor and covet his mate. What for our nature is a sin, would for that one be the norm.

The entire basis of morality, on this account, is the particular nature that we have at the moment. There would be nothing wrong with having a different nature and thus a different natural law. We just don't.

But what if we could? What if we could *change* our nature? According to those who hold this view, we already have. Our ancestors were as different from us, they say, as a prosimian is different from a man. Generation by generation, the ur-men of the long-gone past adapted to a changing environment. Our great-grand-primates were the products of adaptation to a life in the branches of trees. Our grand-primates were the products of adaptation to a life on the savanna. Our parents were the products of adaptation to the practice of agriculture. And our descendants will be the products of adaptation to the most enduring features of our own environment, whatever they may be. Perhaps television.

Notice that on this theory, some of the circumstances to which our ancestors adapted were the results of their prior actions. It was they who came down from the trees, and had therefore to adapt to the savanna. It was they who invented agriculture, and had therefore to adapt to a different diet. In a sense, then, we have been influencing our own evolution all along. We have already changed our nature. We just didn't know that we were doing it.

If there is nothing wrong with having a different nature—and if we have already changed out nature without knowing—then why shouldn't we take the process in hand? Why shouldn't we deliberately change ourselves as we wish to be changed? Why shouldn't we *determine* the nature of our descendants?

Such proposals are no longer idle talk. In October 2000, news leaked that an American company named Biotransplant and an Australian company named Stem Cell Sciences had successfully crossed a human being with a pig by inserting the nuclei of cells from a human fetus into the pigs' eggs. Although the embryos were destroyed when they reached the thirty-two–cell point, they would have continued to grow had they been implanted in the womb of a woman—or a sow.

According to J. Bottum of the *Weekly Standard,* "There has been some suggestion from the creators that their purpose in designing this human pig is to build a new race of subhuman creatures for scientific and medical use. . . . then, too, there has been some suggestion that the creators' purpose is not so much to corrupt humanity as to elevate it." His comments are worth quoting at some length:

> It used to be that even the imagination of this sort of thing ex-
> isted only to underscore a moral in a story. . . . But we live at a
> moment in which British newspapers can report on 19 families who
> have created test-tube babies solely for the purpose of serving as
> tissue donors for their relatives—some brought to birth, some
> merely harvested as embryos and fetuses. A moment in which
> Harper's Bazaar can advise women to keep their faces unwrinkled
> by having themselves injected with fat culled from human cadav-
> ers. . . . In the midst of all this, the creation of a human-pig arrives
> like a thing expected. We have reached the logical end, at last. We
> have become the people that, once upon a time, our ancestors used
> fairy tales to warn their children against—and we will reap exactly
> the consequences those tales foretold. Like the coming true of an
> old story—the discovery of the philosopher's stone, the rubbing
> of a magic lantern—biotechnology is delivering the most aston-
> ishing medical advances anyone has ever imagined. But our sons

and daughters will mate with the pig-men, if the pig-men will have them. And our swine-snouted grandchildren—the fruit not of our loins, but of our arrogance and our bright test tubes—will use the story of our generation to teach a moral to their frightened litters.[4]

Plainly, Bottum is not pleased with what the researchers have done. As he writes, it makes no difference whether they plan to create subhumans or superhumans, for "either they want to make a race of slaves, or they want to make a race of masters. And either way, it means the end of our humanity." The evil is not that the experiment might turn out badly. It is that our nature would be abolished.

But our atheist will ask: What exactly is the objection to abolishing our nature? Why *not* abolish it? We won't be around to mind. Our descendants won't mind either, because we can build into their natures that they are satisfied with the natures they get. If we like, we can make an entire graded set of natures, along the lines of Huxley's *Brave New World.* "I'm glad I'm a Beta," say his Betas. So why *should* we reap the consequences that the tales of old foretold? Why should the pig-men use the story of our generation to teach a moral to their frightened litters? Why should these litters be frightened by what, to them, would be the story of Genesis?

Genesis, I think, is the crux of it. To abolish and remake human nature is to play God. The chief objection to playing God is that someone else is God already. If He created human nature, if he intended it, if it is not the result of a blind fortuity that did not have us in mind— then we have no business exchanging it for another. It would be good to remember that Genesis contains not only the story of creation but the story of Babel, of the presumption of men who thought they could build a tower "to heaven."

Here then is the first difference that the knowledge of God makes to the natural law. A godless natural law would revere the laws of human nature only insofar as we continued to be human. Denying that our humanity is a creation, it would have no reason to preserve this humanity, and no objection to its abolition.

Oughtness. But in what sense can a godless mind revere the laws of human nature at all? The early modern Dutch legal philosopher Hugo Grotius famously remarked that even if there were no God (as he conceded that it would be impious to believe), yet the natural law would have a kind of force.[5] What seems to impress most people who read this remark is that Grotius thinks it *would* have a kind of force. More interesting is his qualifier: It would have a *kind* of force. The suggestion is that it would not have the kind that it would have if God were real.

Taken with that emphasis, the remark of Grotius might be true. Although a godless natural law would lose the force of "oughtness," it would retain the lower force of prudence. But perhaps it would lose that force too. Let us consider further.

The argument for saying that the natural law would lose the force of oughtness but retain the force of prudence runs like this. If there is no God, then the universe is not a creation. One immediate consequence is that I owe nothing to anyone for the fact that I am in it. If there is a reason to keep the moral laws, it cannot lie in honoring the one who made us. Another consequence is that the universe has no meaning beyond itself. The patterns in it *just are*; they do not reflect the goodness or the intentions of a Designer. And this makes a difference, for a theist who attributes the order of nature to God can say (for instance) things like this: "I see that the sexual powers cause conception, and that the fact that they do so is part of the explanation of why human nature has been endowed with such powers in the first place. This tells me that conception is a *purpose* of the sexual powers, a part of what they are *for*. When I employ them, I ought to respect this fact; I ought not to use them in ways that are incompatible with their purpose."

Adding inference to inference in this fashion, he gradually works out a comprehensive account of the right use of the sexual powers and the respect which is owed to the natural institutions which direct and contain them. He can reason similarly about the other natural powers and institutions. Well and good. But an atheist might reply as follows: "I use the word 'purpose' too, and I am even willing to concede that you use it correctly. If one thing causes another, and if this fact is part of the explanation of why the first thing occurs, then the second thing is a purpose of the first[6]; even a Darwinist can concede that much. So what? How do you get from 'B is the purpose of A' to 'I ought not use A in ways that are incompatible with B'? So far as I can see, all that follows from the connection between sex and procreation is that when I do make use of the sexual powers, it would be prudent to watch out."

Stretching a point a bit—taking into account the entire set of things there are to "watch out" for (not only conception, but jealousy, emotional emptiness, loss of trust, and so forth)—perhaps a purely prudential justification of marriage and family and so forth could be developed. And perhaps a purely prudential justification for each of the other natural laws and institutions could also be developed, in the same way. And perhaps that is the sort of thing that Grotius had in mind.

Unfortunately, a truly oughtless prudence would be unable to restrain "free riders." Anyone who thought he saw a way to obtain the benefits of these laws and institutions without their costs—or who was willing to accept the costs of transgressing them—would do so. To speak again of marriage, some men prefer seducing married women. Others say they can do very well without trust. Still others, that although they fear exposure, they would rather risk it than forgo their pleasures. Some even enjoy the risk. For them, it isn't a cost.

To be sure, the oughtless sort of prudence is rather thin. The thicker prudence of the natural law tradition would point out that free riders sacrifice greater goods for lesser ones; they *ought* to desire better for themselves. But they have no *ought*—remember? In their sort of prudence, the good is nothing but the desirable, and the desirable is nothing but what they actually desire. From their point of view, the good for which they feel the greatest desire is the greatest good—just because they feel it.

Arbitrariness. But we have not finished the argument. There is a possible reply. Some would say that the sort of problem I have been describing is a problem only for the naïve atheist, not for the sophisticated sort. With a little more discernment, the person who does not believe in God can reply that as things *just do* have causal and functional properties, so they *just do* have moral properties too. At first this argument seems to save oughtness by sheer fiat. But does it really save anything? In one way, it makes the atheist's case even weaker, because it concedes the arbitrariness of the universe in which he thinks he is living.

Consider the colloquy presented above. Both theist and atheist assumed that the universe is causally patterned: this causes that, that explains this, such-and-such is a reasonable explanation of so-and-so. But what right has the atheist to this assumption? Why should there be any patterns whatsoever? If the universe *just is,* then why shouldn't the things in it *just happen?* There is no reason to expect them to yield to reasoning, no explanation of why they should even have an explanation. Moreover, we are not out of the woods even if we do find patterns in the universe, for if these patterns too *just are,* then there is no warrant for assuming that they are more than local, accidental, superficial, inconsistent, and ephemeral. The sun may not rise tomorrow morning. Fire may not burn this afternoon. Two plus two may equal now four, now six, now one. For me, conception may *not* be caused by sexual intercourse (that is how teenagers think). Even if today I am myself, next week I may be someone else (that is how postmodernists think). So why should the natural law have even the force of prudence, much less oughtness?

Why should there even be logic? Why should I "watch out" for anything? How could I?

But perhaps the only problem with our sophisticated atheist is that he is not sophisticated *enough*. If without God he has no right to assume Pattern, very well: let him be a sort of Platonist, and posit that Pattern itself is God. Of course it would not be what the theist means by God, but it would be God in the impersonal sense: the deepest reality, the underlying principle of everything on which all else depends.

But if he is to be a sort of Platonist, then what does he make of Plato's problem? There are a great many patterns, not just one. This raises the question of what organizes them, binds them all together, in a unity, a Design. We know of only one thing which is capable of Design, and that is mind—intelligent agency. It is not enough for the universe to resemble a mind in *having* design; let us have no tricks, like calling the patterns "ideas" when we have not earned the right to do so. Behind the universe there must be a *real* mind which is capable of designing. That brings us back to God—God as the theist means God, God in the personal sense.[7]

If our atheist accepts this implication, he is back in the fold; he is no longer an atheist. If he denies it—then it would not help him even if Pattern were the deepest reality, because in that case "Pattern" would be merely a fancy name for "patterns," and plurality without Design is merely chaos.

> Turning and turning in the widening gyre
> The falcon cannot hear the falconer;
> Things fall apart; the centre cannot hold;
> Mere anarchy is loosed upon the world.

After all, Plato merely gave names to the ways things hang together; he never explained why they had to hang together. For example he said that all good things participate in a sort of super-pattern, or transcendental, called Goodness, and in token of the fact he assumed an under-lying unity among the virtues—courage, wisdom, justice, moderation, and all the rest. But with nothing to *bring* these good virtues into unity, there is no reason why they should be in unity. Perhaps cowardice is the fount of justice, wisdom comes only to the wanton, and courage makes fools of us all. Perhaps righteousness and peace have not kissed each other, as the Psalmist claims, but tear each other daily into pieces. (And don't many people think this way?) Another of Plato's convictions was that Goodness is but one of the transcendentals; he thought there are two more, Truth and Beauty. That doesn't help matters, it only makes them worse. For why should the three transcendentals hang together? Why shouldn't Goodness be ugly, Beauty lie, and Truth be inimical to the good—not because they *have* come apart, as they seem to in this fallen world, but because they *must* come apart, because that is how they are? Natural selection gives no reason; a clash between, say, Truth and Goodness would not keep an organism from passing on its genes. There *is* no reason—unless there is something else at work, *Someone* else at work, Whom Plato may have known but did not name.

In the end we find that the sophisticated sort of atheist is no better off than the naïve one. His universe is just as mad, and perhaps more terrifying still. It may contain just as much oughtness as he likes, but what ought to be, what charms us, and what *is* are all at war, and the house of Ought is divided against itself.

Moral metastasis. Our question for the last few sections has been what difference it makes to the natural law that we naturally have knowledge of God. So far I have been treating this question as though it meant "What difference would it make to the natural law if we *didn't* have such knowledge?" But there is another way to take it too: "What difference would it make to the natural law if we do have such knowledge but *tell* ourselves we don't?" In other words we may ask about the consequences of lying to ourselves about Him.

Don't we lie to ourselves about ordinary right and wrong? The desire to know truth is ardent, but it is not the only desire at work in us. The desire not to know competes with it desperately, for knowledge is a fearsome thing. So it is that oftentimes we groan about how difficult it is to know what is right even though we know the right perfectly well. Every honest person can confirm this from his own experience. Just how much lying goes on was recently confirmed during the executive branch scandals of the late 1990s, when everyone from television interviewer Geraldo Rivera to comedian Jerry Seinfeld seemed to agree that "Everybody lies about sex." As Seinfeld put it in an August 5, 1998, interview with Michael Blowen of the *Boston Globe,* "Truth and sex don't go together. . . . truth just isn't going to happen." I take him to have been talking not just about our lying to other people but about our lying to ourselves, because one can't do that much lying without rationalizing it to himself somehow.

But the problem of lying to ourselves goes far beyond sex. Along with the main axis of the natural law tradition, I have suggested that one of the things about reality and goodness that we know perfectly well is the reality and goodness of God. Biblical tradition agrees: when Psalm 14 remarks "The fool says in his heart 'There is no God'," it doesn't call him a fool for thinking it, but for saying it even though yet deeper in his mind he knows it isn't true. From this point of view, the reason it is so difficult to argue with an atheist—as I know, having been one—is that he is not being honest with himself. He knows that there is a God; he only tells himself that he doesn't.

You don't have to take this from a theist like me. Consider the remarks of the Harvard population biologist Richard Lewontin—an atheist who thinks matter is all there is—in the *New York Review of Books*:

> Our willingness to accept scientific claims that are against common sense is the key to an understanding of the real struggle between science and the supernatural. We take the side of science *in*

spite of the patent absurdity of some of its constructs, *in spite of* its failure to fulfill many of its extravagant promises of health and life, *in spite of* the tolerance of the scientific community for unsubstantiated just-so stories, because we have a prior commitment, a commitment to materialism. It is not that the methods and institutions of science somehow compel us to accept a material explanation of the phenomenal world but, on the contrary, that we are forced by our a priori adherence to material causes to create an apparatus of investigation and a set of concepts that produce material explanations, no matter how counterintuitive, no matter how mystifying to the uninitiated. Moreover, that materialism is absolute, for we cannot allow a divine foot in the door.[8]

Lewontin is admitting that he and those who think like him are only selective skeptics. They are hostile to belief in God because of an a priori commitment to a dogmatism which excludes God—a dogmatism about which they are not skeptical at all, which they accept not because of the evidence but in spite of it, and to which they will cling even when it forces them into absurdities.

For another example, consider the remarks of the philosopher Thomas Nagel in his book *The Last Word*. The purpose of the book is to defend philosophical rationalism against subjectivism. At a certain point Nagel acknowledges that rationalism has theistic implications. For the moment, the important thing is not whether that is true (although I have already argued that it is), but that Nagel thinks that it is. What is important is what he says next. After suggesting that contemporary subjectivism may be due to "fear of religion," he cites his own fear of religion as a case in point. In his own words: "I speak from experience, being strongly subject to this fear myself: I want atheism to be true and am made uneasy by the fact that some of the most intelligent and well-informed people I know are religious believers. It isn't just that I don't believe in God and, naturally, hope that I'm right in my belief. It's that I hope there is no God! I don't want there to be a God; I don't want the universe to be like that." He adds, "My guess is that this cosmic authority problem is not a rare condition and that it is responsible for much of the scientism and reductionism of our time. One of the tendencies it supports is the ludicrous overuse of evolutionary biology to explain everything about life, including everything about the human mind. Darwin enabled modern secular culture to heave a great collective sigh of relief, by apparently providing a way to eliminate purpose, meaning, and design as fundamental features of the world."[9]

If Nagel is right, then those who say that theism is a crutch have got it backwards. For our contemporary intellectual culture, it is atheism that serves as a crutch. It couldn't have been easy to admit that.

So it seems that these men come close to agreeing with me. To be sure they don't agree that God is real. But they agree that there is something not quite honest in their rejection of Him—something dogmatically driven, as in Lewontin's case, or emotionally driven, as in Nagel's— rather than forced upon them by the evidence. The view that the atheist is not being honest with himself—that He knows that there is a God, but only tells himself he doesn't know—is looking better and better.

If this preposterous view is true—as I think it is—then it changes everything. For then the important question is not "Is there a God?", but "Can I concede one part of my moral knowledge while holding down another?", or "Can I admit to myself that I know about, say, the goodness of love and the evil of murder, while *not* admitting to myself that I know about the goodness of God and the evil of refusing Him?"

One certainly can do that—lots of agnostics do—but one can never do it well. An agnostic claims ignorance about God. If he concedes that it is *possible* to know something about God but that he does not know it, then he condemns himself, for he is too lazy to learn the most important thing. To justify himself he would have to maintain that knowledge of God is *not* the most important thing, but that would be merely to claim that something else is God—and that he already knows all about it. If he says that it is *impossible* to know anything about God, he contradicts himself, for to know God's unknowability would be to know something about God. Indeed, it would be to know a great deal about Him. First, one would have to assume that He is infinitely distant, because otherwise one could not be so sure that knowledge about Him is impossible. Second, one would have to assume that He is unconcerned, because otherwise one would expect Him to have provided the means for one to know Him. Finally, one would have to assume that He is completely unlike the portrayal of Him in the Bible, because in that account He does care about us and has already provided the means for us to know Him. So in the end the so-called agnostic must claim to know quite a number of things about God. The problem is he cannot justify any of them.

The gambit of claiming "I don't know" slips from one's control because, at bottom, it is a lie, and lies metastasize; the universe is so tightly constructed that in order to cover up one lie, we must usually tell another. This applies with just as much force to the lies we tell ourselves as to the lies we tell to other people. One could imagine a universe so loosely-jointed that lies did not require the support of more lies, but the one we live in is not like that. In this one, deception begets deception, and self-deception begets more self-deception; the greater the lie, the greater its metastatic tendency. This tendency is strongest precisely in the case of the greatest self-deception, pretending not to know that God is real, because there are so many things one must *not think of* in order to not think of the reality of God.

One cannot predict in advance *what* stories one will tell himself to make believe that he does not know the reality of God and his obligation to Him; every agnostic and atheist devises a different set of plausibility gambits, a different pattern of omissions, of forgettings, of avertings of gaze. But it is extraordinarily difficult—I think impossible—for such self-deceptions not to slop over at some point into what he admits about the moral law. You may try to be truthful about the goodness of loving your neighbor—but if you lie to yourself about the God who loved your neighbor into being, then your understanding of all love and every neighbor will be defective. A more adequate understanding of love and neighbor will be very dangerous, because it may make you think of God.

The previous sections were about the logical connectedness of the knowledge of God with the knowledge of the rest of moral law. This section has been about their psychological connectedness. There are things we can't not know—but there are also things we can't not do. Our minds won't go like that.

THE SECOND PART OF THE INQUIRY

The next part of the inquiry is what difference it makes to accept biblical revelation *over and above* the natural knowledge of God. How—for those who accept it—does the divine law *illuminate* the natural?

Forgiveness again. C. S. Lewis once wrote that man has two clues to the meaning of the universe. One is the knowledge of a law that he did not make but is obligated to keep; the other is the knowledge that he does not and cannot keep it. This is why I remarked earlier that a clear vision of the moral law reveals a debt which exceeds anything we can pay. Apart from an assurance that the debt can be forgiven—something available only in biblical revelation because it transcends what human reason can find out on its own—no human being dares to face the law straight-on.

Yet we can't quite wipe the law from our intellects. It seems to be woven into the deep structure of our minds, as experts on linguistics say the threads of language are. Unable to make it go away, we use every means we can devise to pretend that we are really being good. Evasions and rationalizations spread through our intellects like the mycelium of a fungus in its host. That is why the ancient world was brutal, as we of all people should understand. Not even the greatest of the pagans could admit what was wrong with infanticide, although they knew that the child was of our kind. Neither can we admit what is wrong with abortion and a host of other evils.

It is hard enough to face the moral law even *with* the revelation that divine justice and divine mercy are conjoined. It offends our pride to be forgiven, terrifies it to surrender control. Without the possibility of forgiveness, how could we ever bear to face how wrong we had been about anything, how could we ever bear to change our minds? The history of ethics would be a history of digging in against plain truths. Consider how many centuries it took natural law thinkers, even in the Christian tradition, to work out the implications of the brotherhood of master and slave. At least they did eventually. Outside of the biblical orbit, no one ever did—not spontaneously.

It may seem that the possibility of forgiveness matters only on the assumption that there is, in fact, a God—that without the lawgiver, there would be no law, and therefore nothing to be forgiven. The actual state of affairs is more dreadful, for the Furies of conscience do not wait upon our assumptions. One who acknowledges the Furies but denies the God who appointed them—who supposes that there *can* be a law without a lawgiver—must suppose that forgiveness is both necessary and impossible. That which is not personal cannot forgive; morality "by itself" has a heart of rock. And so although grace would be unthinkable, the ache for it would keen on, like a cry in a deserted street.

Providence. Self-interest is not the only thing that tempts us to commit injustice. One of the strongest motives to do wrong is to make everything go right. For sometimes justice requires allowing bad things to happen to other people. If we forbid hanging innocent men, the mob may break out in a riot. If we forbid targeting noncombatants for bombing, the war may be prolonged. If we forbid giving perjured testimony, the murderer may go unpunished. Surely it isn't right, we reason, that there are riots, longer wars, and murderers free in the streets. Let us do evil for the sake of good. It doesn't seem just to do justice.

Christian faith undercuts the urge to fix everything on our own, through conviction of the final helplessness of man and confidence in the providence of God—through certainty that only God can set everything to rights, and faith that in the end, He will. Man can only ameliorate, not cure. But there will be a Judgment, and there will be a hand that wipes every tear from the eyes of those who mourn.

The final helplessness of man to fix himself may seem fatuously obvious after a century which killed hundreds of millions of people, all with the idea of improving human life. If it is a fatuity, however, it is unbearable fatuity, one that we persistently refuse to accept. I commented earlier on the idea that one *may* play God if there is no Creator. What we have in view here is the conviction that one *must* play God if the Creator is not a Judge and Healer too. Immanuel Kant thought that morality would be undermined without a belief in divine judgment, but Kant did not know the half of it. The wrongs of the world would not merely dismay the desire to do right. They would taunt, torture, and drive men to a despair which could be relieved only by committing yet greater wrongs, on the principle that if God is not our Savior then we must save ourselves.[10]

There may be some few who could resist this terrible conclusion. I have not met them. It is no accident that not even the Stoics, who invented the very term "natural law," ever rose to the idea of principles which hold without exception, principles which may not be violated even to prevent violations. The problem was not that they failed to find these principles written upon their hearts, but that they could not bring themselves to attend closely to the inscription. It would have been too awful to believe that the goodness of the ends did not justify the wickedness of the means, because how else could the ends be achieved? The same people who said *Fiat justitia ruat caelum,* "Let justice be done, though the heavens fall," also said *Salus populi suprema lex,* "The safety of the people is the supreme law"—and as they understood these mottoes, the second undid the first. Have the Germans begun another uprising? Then raze their villages, rape their virgins, and show them what the *Pax Romana* means. All for justice, all for order, all for peace.

Without confidence in providence, our vision of every Commandment goes askew. The Fifth, for example, seems to change before our eyes from "You shall not kill" to "You must keep as many alive as possible"—at the expense of others, if that is what it takes. In the movie *Sophie's Choice,* a Nazi guard at Auschwitz commands the young mother to choose which of her children will be sent to the ovens. If she cooperates in the crime, the one she selects will be burned; if she refuses, then both of them will be taken to their deaths. After a slow, hanging moment, she pushes away her smallest child and cries out that he take that one—not the other! Not her favorite! Her choice is plainly evil; for the sake of a better result, she has united herself with the sin of the murderer. And in the end the other child dies too. But how could she choose otherwise, if she had no faith in God?

When I asked some of my graduate students to discuss the story, I was astonished to hear one argue that it would have been "selfish" for Sophie to refuse to mark one of her children for death. How could it be selfish? Because, he said, she should have been willing to "sacrifice herself"—by which he meant *to sacrifice her conscience.* It took me some time to realize that my student, an agnostic, considered "I must promote life" to be a real moral duty, but viewed "I must not kill" as a mere scruple, an item of personal identity, on a par with "I am not the sort of person who skips bathing." He didn't deny that conscience speaks differently; he only thought it was a liar. For the sake of a better result, he said, Sophie should have been willing to suffer the agonies of its accusations.

And if there is no God, why not? The motto "Do the right thing and let God take care of the consequences" makes sense only on the assurance that He will take care of the consequences. Without that assurance, doing the right thing *means* taking care of the consequences—

or trying to. And so unless there is providence, the urge to do good irresistibly consorts with evil. Unless God is just, *our* justice becomes unhinged.

The Image of God.[11] To be a person is to be a proper subject of absolute regard—a "neighbor" in the sense of the Commandments—a being of the sort whom the Commandments are about. It is *persons* whom I am not to kill, *persons* whom I am to love as I love myself. But what is a person? If we accept the biblical revelation that man is the *imago Dei,* the image of God, then every human being is a person—a person by nature, a kind of thing different from any other kind, a being whose very existence is a kind of sacrament, a sign of God's grace. Trying to understand man without recognizing him as the *imago Dei* is like trying to understand a bas-relief without recognizing it as a carving.

The problem with rejecting this biblical revelation is not that one loses the dim, inbuilt sense of awe that clings to human life. The problem is that this inbuilt sense is not enough. We need an explanation of what it is that we are sensing when we experience the sense of awe. Without the explanation, I may try to hold onto your knowledge of the evil of murdering my neighbor, but I will find it difficult to recognize my neighbor when I see him. It is not impossible. More or less adequate explanations *can* be constructed from materials accessible to natural reason. But that is the long way around, and most people weary long before they reach the end of it. For the most part, the ones who do stay on the trail are the same ones who acknowledge the biblical revelation of the *imago Dei.*

In contemporary secular ethics, the ruling tendency is to concede that there are such things as persons, but to define them in terms of their functions or capacities—not by what they *are,* the image of God, but by what they can *do.* To give but a single well-known illustration, philosopher Mary Ann Warren defines "personhood" in terms of consciousness, reasoning, self-motivated activity, the capacity to communicate about indefinitely many topics, and conceptual self-awareness. If you can do all those things, you're a person; if you can't, you're not.[12] The functional approach to personhood seems plausible at first, just because—at a certain stage of development, and barring misfortune—most persons do have these functions. But Warren thinks persons *are* their functions, and this error blows the core right out of the moral code.

Warren herself is a case in point. She offers her definition to justify abortion. Obviously, unborn babies are not capable of reasoning, complex communication, and so on. If they cannot perform these functions, then by Warren's definition they aren't persons, and if they aren't persons, they have no inherent right to life. But it cannot end there. If unborn babies may be killed because they lack these functions, then a great many other individuals may also be killed for the same reasons—for example the asleep, unconscious, demented, addicted, and very young, not to mention sundry other cases such as deaf-mutes who have not been taught sign language. In Warren's language, none of these are persons; in biblical language, she refuses to recognize her neighbors. She does claim to oppose infanticide—but only because any given infant is probably wanted by someone. The infant is still not a neighbor to her; she does not concede that it has an *inherent* claim to our regard. If no one does happen to want it, then "its destruction is permissible."[13]

The cure for such blindness is not to tinker with the list of functions by which we define persons, but to stop confusing what persons are with what they can typically do. Can this be done without recourse to the biblical teaching about the *imago Dei*? Yes, but unlike the biblical revelation itself, the argument is highly technical and flies over most people's heads. Not only that, but it raises further questions which we cannot answer without returning to the *imago Dei*. Let us see how.

The key is to ask "For what kinds of things are functional definitions appropriate?" They are appropriate for things which have no inherent nature, whose identity is dependent on our purposes and interests—things which do not intrinsically deserve to be regarded in a certain

way, but which may be regarded in any way which is convenient. For
example, suppose I am building an automobile and I need to keep two
moving parts from touching each other. I don't need an object of a particular natural kind for that. Anything can be a spacer which fills the
space—anything which has the property of being able to keep the two
components from touching. But that implies that the spacer is a function of *my* need to keep the other two components apart. The particular lump of matter I use to accomplish this purpose is not intrinsically
a proper subject of absolute regard; my regard for it—even its very identity as a spacer—is relative to how I want to use it, or to what I find
interesting about it.

By contrast, if I am a person then I am *by nature* a rights-bearer, *by
nature* a proper subject of absolute regard—not because of what I can
do, but because of what I am. Of course this presupposes that I *have* a
nature, a "what-I-am," which is distinct from the present condition or
stage of development of what I am, distinct from my abilities in that
condition or stage of development, and, in particular, distinct from how
this condition, stage of development, or set of abilities might happen
to be valued by other people. In short, a person is *by nature* someone
whom it is wrong to view merely functionally—wrong to value merely
as a means to the ends or the interests of others. If you regard me as a
person only because I am able to exercise certain capacities that interest you, then you are saying that I am an object of your regard not in an
absolute but only in a relative sense. You are saying that I am a person
not for what I am, but for what I can do; not for what I deserve, but for
what you happen to respect. In fact you are saying that I am *not* a person. And so the functional definition of personhood does not even rise
to the dignity of being wrong. It is incoherent.

Some modern people will bite the bullet and agree with me. They
will try to rescue their position not by drawing back, but by pushing
further still, becoming "post" modern. "Very well!" they might say. "Let
us grant that persons in the merely functionally sense are not persons

in the moral sense. But in that case there *are* no moral persons, because the 'human beings' whom *you* call moral persons do not exist. There are no 'natural kinds.' There are no 'natures.' There is no 'what-I-am.' All value is relative, because all meaning is relative; all meaning is relative, because every definition is contrived to the convenience of the definer. The definition of the 'human' is no less contrived than any other."

They have a point. We saw earlier that without God, there is no reason to believe in any sort of pattern in things—'natures' included. Alas, their way of thinking escapes the previous incoherency only to fall into a greater one. The former incoherency concerned only how we think of persons. The new one concerns how we think of everything—how we think of reality, how we think of thinking. A condition of being able to say anything meaningful at all is that *not* everything is a creature of our own regard for it. There must exist some things that are what they are despite us; their meanings provide the anchors for all other meanings. If all meaning were relative, then even the meanings of the terms in the proposition "All meaning is relative" would be relative. Therefore the proposition "All meaning is relative" destroys itself. It is nothing but an evasion of reality. That seems a high price to pay, even for the privilege of killing people.

A modernist who rejects the greater of these incoherencies is not yet in the clear; one does not have to believe that all meanings slip away to see the meaning of the person slip away. Though a modernist may keep up the pretense that he is still talking about what persons really are, his method allows him to know only what he wants them to be—and different modernists want them to be different things. One thinker has greater regard for sentience, another for cognition, another for self-awareness. One thinks the important thing is sociality, another the capacity to make plans. With each different criterion of personhood, a different set of beings is welcomed through the gates of others' regard. This writer says that higher mammals are persons, but human babies not. That one says that human babies are persons, but Grandma not.

The one over there says that *some* human babies are persons, but only if their mothers think they are.[14] The weakest and most helpless, who were once held to have the highest claim on our protection, are now held to have the least.

Denial of the *imago Dei* is something new, and much more dangerous than a simple return to paganism. As Francis Schaeffer once remarked, the worst that could be said of the pagans was that they had not yet heard that man is made in the image of God. Although they naturally recognized the dignity of man and the justice that is due to him, their understanding of this intuition was deficient. By contrast, our thinkers have heard that man is made in the image of God, *but deny it.* This puts such a strain on the inbuilt structures of moral knowledge that justice flips upside down. Refusing to learn, they finally distort even what they already know.

PART II

EXPLAINING THE LOST WORLD

Some things we need to know
about our misplaced moral knowledge.

4

The First and Second Witnesses

Two natural sources of moral knowledge: the witness
of deep conscience, and the witness of design as such.

CLASSICAL EDUCATION TAUGHT ITS PUPILS that there was some real moral knowledge in the universal common sense of plain people; the task was not to get free of it but to refine it. By contrast, modern education teaches its pupils to distance themselves from this common moral sense, to call it not knowledge but "belief." A person of modern education wants to know how we know before deciding what we know; he demands a critique of the faculty of knowing before conceding that he knows anything at all.

This suspicion is partly reasonable and partly unreasonable. The reasonable part is that up to a point, we can certainly investigate how we know things. The unreasonable part is that in order to do so, we have to know something already—otherwise we have no equipment for the investigation. There must be some first principles that are not derived from other principles, some first knowledge that comes to us without prior investigation. It isn't because someone has taught us ethics that we know we have duties toward other people, and if we didn't already know it, we couldn't be taught ethics.

KNOWING HOW WE KNOW

Not all of natural law is "first" knowledge. But the most fundamental part of it is, and this is the part that troubles modern people most. In the case of first knowledge, the investigation of how we know is mostly descriptive. For example, we can say *that there is* first knowledge of morality—that is descriptive. We can also tell what belongs to it—friendship is good, gratuitous harm is wrong, we ought to be fair, and so on. We can even give a name to the way we have first moral knowledge—the usual name is "conscience." Beyond that, however, the investigation is mostly negative. *How* conscience tells us that we ought to be fair, nobody knows. This we can say: we don't know it just from being told, we don't know it from the five senses, and we don't know it by inference from prior knowledge. We just know it. The knowledge is "underived."

In the case of derived or "second" moral knowledge, we can sometimes go a little further, and I will discuss three different ways that we derive it. Even here, though, not everything about how people derive their knowledge can be analyzed. If we reason that the best explanation for P is Q, how do we recognize Q as the best explanation? Or if we reason that P presupposes Q, how do we recognize Q as a presupposition? Sometimes we can answer this question, but sometimes not; we just recognize it. By the way, it isn't just in morality that we find this to be the case. How do we know that we exist? No one knows. Not so, you say. I think, therefore I exist. But how do you know that you think? No one knows that either. You just do.

The language of "first" and "second" knowledge should not be misunderstood. "First" does not mean first in time, but deeper in the order of presuppositions. No one decides whether to cross the street by reasoning from first principles. The point is that if we asked someone why he crossed the street, and he gave a reason . . . asked him why *that* was a good reason, and he gave a reason . . . asked him why *that* was a good reason, and he gave a reason . . . eventually he would reach first principles, and then he could go no further.

There are at least four different ways that "what we can't not know" is known. In the spirit of Paul, these might be called witnesses[1]: the witness of deep conscience, the witness of design as such, the witness of our own design, and the witness of natural consequences. I present the former two briefly in this chapter, and the latter two at greater length in the next. The discussion of conscience is especially brief, because its terrible workings are discussed in more detail later in the book.

THE WITNESS OF DEEP CONSCIENCE

The older natural law thinkers had two different words for conscience, reflecting a real difference between two aspects of the moral intellect— a difference that we have forgotten. *Synderesis,*[2] or deep conscience, is the interior witness to the foundational principles of moral law. *Conscientia,*[3] or surface conscience, is conscious moral belief, especially about the upper stories of moral law. It is what we derive *from* the foundational principles, whether correctly or incorrectly, by means honest or dishonest.

There is a small difficulty about what to call everyday moral rules which are both known to everyone and right for everyone, but which, strictly speaking, are derived. Thomas Aquinas put even the prohibition of murder in this category: It is derived from a still more fundamental principle—the wrong of gratuitous harm—but its derivation is so immediate and obvious that the precept is scarcely distinguishable from first knowledge, and for practical purposes is equally foundational. I call such rules the "belt" of *synderesis.* Deep conscience, then, includes both *synderesis* and the belt of *synderesis.*

Surface conscience presents greater possibilities for going wrong. It can be erased, it can be mistaken, and it can vary from person to person. In fact it can blur and err in at least nine different ways[4]: One way is insufficient experience, where I don't know enough to reach sound conclusions; another is insufficient skill, where I have never learned the art of reasoning well. Then come sloth, where I am too lazy to reason, and corrupt custom, where it has never occurred to me to do so. Next come passion, where I am distracted by strong feeling from reasoning carefully, and fear, where I am afraid to reason because I might find out that I am wrong. Bringing up the rear are wishful thinking, where I include in my reasoning only what I am willing to notice; depraved ideology, where I interpret known principles crookedly; and malice, where I refuse to reason because I am determined to do what I want. Yet underneath all of the resulting false convictions is a testimony gripping, profound, and true, however it may have been twisted and falsified on its path into present awareness. This is the witness of deep conscience.

By contrast with surface conscience, deep conscience cannot be erased, cannot be mistaken, and is the same in every human being. The only way to tamper with it is self-deception—telling myself that I don't know what I really do. All natural law thinkers agree that it includes the knowledge of inviolable goods like friendship,[5] of formal norms like fairness, and of everyday moral rules like "Do not murder." The disagreements turn on more technical points. Some think that the basic goods and formal norms lie deepest in the mind, and the everyday moral rules are derived from them. Others think that it is the other way around: the everyday moral rules lie deepest in the mind, and awaken us to the basic goods and formal rules. Still others think the basic goods, formal norms, and everyday moral rules lie equally deep in the mind, and illuminate each other. At issue is what belongs strictly to *synderesis* and what belongs to its belt. This puzzle need not detain us. It is not clear how such a disagreement could be settled, or even whether settling it is important. The crucial thing is that at whatever respective depths they lie, the knowledge of basic goods, of formal norms, and of everyday moral rules are all found in deep conscience.

Deep conscience is the reason why even a man who tells himself there is no right and wrong may shrink from committing murder; why even a man who murders may suffer the pangs of remorse; and why even a man who has deadened himself to remorse shows other symptoms of deep-buried guilty knowledge. By other symptoms of guilty knowledge I do not mean guilty feelings, because no one always feels guilty for doing wrong, and some people never do. We sometimes imagine that to lack guilty feelings is to lack a conscience, but deep conscience is knowledge, not feelings, and guilty knowledge darkly asserts itself regardless of the state of the feelings. A pro-abortion journalist quotes a pro-abortion counselor as commenting, "I am not confident even now, with abortion so widely used, that women feel it's OK to want an abortion without feeling guilty. They say, 'Am I some sort of monster that I feel all right about this?'"[6] The statement is revealing. Plainly, if a woman has guilty feelings for *not* having guilty feelings, she must have guilty knowledge. I leave these matters now because we will return to them in chapter seven.

THE WITNESS OF DESIGN AS SUCH

In the previous section we considered the witness of deep conscience. But why should we care what conscience tells us? Why should we consider it a "witness" at all? What if its "witness" is a lie? For example, what if our genes evolved without direction, we are blindly programmed for their preservation, and conscience is one of the programs—a means of directing us by remote control? Zoologist Richard Dawkins thinks so. "We are survival machines," he says, "robot vehicles blindly programmed to preserve the selfish molecules known as genes."[7] In that case, it might be argued that a wise man would bend his energies to finding a way to turn off the remote. Dawkins thinks that too. "Let us understand what our own selfish genes are up to," he writes, "because we may then at least have the chance to upset their designs, something that no other species has ever aspired to."[8] After all, unless deep conscience is *designed* to tell us truth, there is no particular reason why it should. And so a presupposition of regarding deep conscience as a witness—as we all, deep down, know it is—is that it has been designed to tell us truth by someone wise enough to do so.

But is this plausible? It is more than plausible. For a short hundred and fifty years, it was the boast of the Darwinists that living things only *seem* to be designed—in particular, that "man is the result of a meaningless and purposeless process that did not have us in mind."[9] Today we have overwhelming evidence that this is not so. Living things contain immense and irreducible complexity that cannot be accounted for by the mechanism that Darwin proposed. Natural selection is supposed to proceed by undirected small modifications, one bit at a time, but the living cell has turned out to be a maze of molecular machines, in many of which the parts interact in such a way that unless all of them are present *at once*, the machine either doesn't work right, or doesn't work at all.[10] There could be no selective advantage in having one part, or two parts, or three, because these machines do not function at all until their assembly is complete. Darwin wrote that "If it could be demonstrated that any complex organ existed which could not possibly have been formed by numerous, successive, slight modifications, my theory would absolutely break down."[11] By his own criterion, then, his theory has absolutely broken down.

Even if human beings could have come about by natural selection, the Darwinian mechanism does not explain where life came from in the first place. Even if it could explain where life came from in the first place, it doesn't explain where the universe came from. And even if it could explain where the universe came from, it doesn't explain why the universe is exquisitely fine-tuned for the possibility of life like us. These things are so plain that even an atheist like the Nobel Prize-winning astrophysicist Fred Hoyle was forced to recognize them:

From 1953 onward, Willy Fowler and I have always been intrigued by the remarkable relation of the 7.65 Mev energy level in the nucleus of 12 C to the 7.12 Mev level in 16 O. If you wanted to produce carbon and oxygen in roughly equal quantities by stellar nucleosynthesis, these are the two levels you would have to fix, and your fixing would have to be just where these levels are actually found to be. Another put-up job? Following the above argument, I am inclined to think so. A common sense interpretation of the facts suggests that a superintellect has monkeyed with physics, as well as with chemistry and biology, and that there are no blind forces worth speaking about in nature.[12]

If we say "monkeyed with by a superintellect" I think we may as well go on to say "designed by God." Of course there are ways to avoid this conclusion; the question is whether they are plausible.

For example, some people (Hoyle among them) have claimed that extraterrestrial civilizations must have seeded earth with prefabricated genes—everything which the evolution of intelligent life would require. But then you must ask how the extraterrestrial civilizations came to be. Besides, it is not enough to seed the planet with genetic ready-mix. What kind of extraterrestrials could have "monkeyed with" the laws of physics? Or you can follow the former Harvard biochemist George Wald, who admitted that the odds are against life arising, but thought that given enough time, "the 'impossible' becomes possible, the possible probable, and the probable virtually certain."[13] The problem here is that the time available for life to have arisen is getting shorter and shorter. Wald himself thought two billion years had passed between the time the oceans stopped boiling and the time life appeared. New estimates suggest that his guess was forty times too long. But you can be even more extravagant than Wald. Rather than saying that given enough *time* the impossible becomes possible, you can say the trick is to have enough *universes*. If there are an infinite number of them, then intelligent life will arise in some of them even if the odds against are astronomically high. You can even suppose that each universe has slightly different physical laws; that way, in some of them the odds against might *not* be astronomically high. But this is really going too far. In order to avoid believing in just one God we are now asked to believe in an infinite number of universes, all of them unobservable just because they are not part of ours. The principle of inference seems to be not Occam's Razor but Occam's Beard: "Multiply entities unnecessarily."

Besides, why should any universes exist? Why even one? Why should there be any laws of physics whatsoever? Such things do not explain themselves. Even a child recognizes that anything which *might not have been* requires a cause. Philosophers call such things "contingent beings." But the universe—an ensemble of contingent beings—is itself a contingent being, so the universe itself must have a cause. Now if we say that the cause of the universe is another contingent being, we merely invite an infinite regress. For the regress to have an end, we must eventually reach a being which is not contingent but necessary—not something which might not have been, but something which *can't not be*. Furthermore this necessary being must be sufficient to cause its effects, and so it must have all of the qualities traditionally ascribed to God: Eternity, power, and all the rest.

I have written this section in reverse. It is not by molecular machines and carbon-oxygen ratios that we know that God is real. Nor is it by criticizing abstruse speculations about extraterrestrials, about the age of the universe, or about universes other than our own. The knowledge of God belongs to us already; these arguments are not its source, but only responses to objections. We recognize immediately that nature requires an explanation beyond itself, that the things in nature are designed, that design requires personal agency. In short, we recognize immediately that we are created by the one true God.

There is more: "He has set eternity in the hearts of men." Not only has He designed us to know about Him, but He has designed us to long for Him, reverence Him, and adore Him.[14] On occasion, even atheists are overpowered by the sensations of gratitude, of the presence of God, and of Godward longing. Their burden is that they have no explanation for why any such feeling should exist, and must try to attach them to other things than God.[15] Certainly such sensations have no survival value. Sociobiologist E. O. Wilson has suggested that "a gene" for religiosity would help human groups hold together,[16] but religion can divide groups just as easily as it unites them. If holding together is what enables us to survive, then why hasn't natural selection simply produced a gene for holding together? The best explanation for the *sensus divinitatis* is that we were designed by the Divinity to have it.

The mere recognition of design does three things for our moral knowledge. First, it vindicates deep conscience. If *synderesis* is designed as a witness to moral truth by a God who knows what He is doing, then its witness to this truth is reliable. Second, it confirms that we have duties not only to neighbor but to God Himself, to whom we owe the very possibility of the experience of anything good. Third, it informs us that just as deep conscience is designed, so the rest of us is designed; we are a canvass for His purposes.

Philosopher William A. Dembski observes that "Design" is a better name for a research program than for a theory. Once we realize that something is designed—whether us or another thing—our questions have only begun. What are the components of the design? What is the function of each one? What degree of disturbance allows it to go on functioning? Once it has been disturbed, how can the original function be recovered? What are the constraints within which it functions well, but outside of which it breaks? What were the designer's intentions?[17]

Engineers are used to asking such questions. So are physicians. Although natural law thinkers ought to be, we are far from that point at present. Some things are plain, however, and to a few of the features of our own design we now turn.

5

The Third and Fourth Witnesses

*The other two natural sources of moral knowledge:
the witness of our own design, and the witness of natural
consequences. Concluding thoughts about the four witnesses.*

TO MAKE PROPER USE of something that has been designed, we
have to know how it works. That means knowing how each
feature contributes to the fulfillment of its functions. In the
body, the heart is for pumping blood; each valve, nerve, chamber and
vessel does its part to move the blood along. Every doctor understands
this; no sensible surgeon tries to make the heart pump air instead of
blood. The reason is simple: when you thwart a thing's design, it no
longer does what it is supposed to do. It either works badly, stops working, or breaks. Something goes terribly wrong.

These things can be observed, and so become another source of
moral knowledge. Because every part of us has meaning, our very bodies have a language of their own; they say things by what we do with
them. Bone speaks to bone, organ to organ, skin to skin. A smile means
something friendly; you cannot give that meaning to a slap in the face.
You can use a kiss to betray, but only because the kiss, in itself, means
something else. Conjugal sex means self-giving, making one flesh out
of two. By contrast, when a man puts the part of himself which repre-

sents new life into the cavity of another man which represents decay and expulsion, at the most basic of all possible levels he is saying "Life, be swallowed in death."[1] We cannot overwrite such meanings with different ones just because we want to.

Design is obvious not just in our bodies but across the whole range of human powers and capacities. The function of fear is to warn; of minds, to deliberate and know; of anger, to prepare for the protection of endangered goods. Everything in us has a purpose; everything is *for* something. A power is well-used when it is used for that purpose and according to that design. Thus the virtue of courage is not being fearless, but fearing rightly: For the right reasons, in the right way, and to the right degree, neither more nor differently.

THE WITNESS OF OUR OWN DESIGN

Some of the most interesting features of our moral design show up not at the level of the individual but at the level of the species. The four most striking are interdependence, complementarity, spontaneous order, and subsidiarity. As to the first three, some manifestations are so obvious that no human being overlooks them; others are more subtle, and easily missed. The fourth is evident only on reflection, but as a corollary of two other principles which are somewhat more plain. In our species design, then, we find a mix of things we can't not know and things we can.

Interdependency. We are certainly not hive creatures, but we are not self-sufficient either. In fact, the modes of our interdependency are legion. To mention just a few: We depend on each other physically, for we are not automatically provided with food, warmth, and the means of escape or protection as the other animals are; no one can provide all these things to himself, nor can anyone do much to help himself when he is gravely injured or ill. We depend on each other intellectually, for it is by reasoning together that we find out what we need and how to obtain it, not to mention what we should live for and how. We depend on each other developmentally, for we take much longer than other creatures to reach maturity, and on the way we require discipline and instruction by others in the use of our powers. We depend on each other procreatively, for we neither divide like amoebas, bud like yeast, nor conceive without mates like certain species of mosquitos; nor is mating the end of it, for parents cooperate both in nurturing their offspring and in helping them establish their own families. We depend on each other for identity, for even though we are distinct from each other, each understands who he is in part through understanding how others see him and in relation to his group. We depend on each other morally, for each person is accountable to the others, and the development of virtue is a partnership in goodness rather than a solitary pursuit. At last we depend on each other politically, for although some requirements of the common good are best supplied privately, others require coordination by authority. Chief among these is public justice, for no man can judge rightly in his own case.

I have said nothing of our dependence on God, or of how we were made to depend on each other spiritually. These matters too concern the human design—not in itself, but as a preparation for grace. But they exceed what can be known apart from direct revelation.[2]

Complementarity. Not only do we depend on each other, but we depend on each other in a particular way. One illustration is found in the natural diversity of our bents and abilities, which is the basis for the division of labor. People of different crafts and vocations, like merchant and producer, inventor and entrepreneur, teacher and practitioner, depend on each other not so much in the way that one finger lends strength to another, but in the way that the fingers complement the thumb—opposing each other so as to grasp. Their differences are precisely what enable them to work together.

An even stronger illustration is found in the natural difference between the sexes, which is the basis for the division of roles in the family. Short of a divine provision for people called to celibacy, there is something missing in the man which must be provided by the woman, and something missing in the woman which must be provided by the man. This is most obvious in the physical dimension. In the case of all other biological functions, only one body is required to do the job. A person can digest food by himself, using no other gullet but his own; he can see by himself, using no other eyes but his own; he can walk by himself, using no other legs but his own; and so with each of the other functions and their corresponding organs. Each of us can perform every vital function by himself, except one. The single exception is procreation. What this demonstrates is that among human beings the male and female sexual powers are radically incomplete, and designed for each other. If we were speaking of respiration, it would be as though the man had the diaphragm, the woman the lungs, and they had to come together to take a single breath. If we were speaking of circulation, it would be as though the man had the right heart chambers, the woman the left, and they had to come together to make a single beat. Now it isn't like that with the respiratory or circulatory powers, but that is exactly how it is with the generative powers. The union of opposites is the only possible realization of their procreative potential; unless they come together as a single organism, as one flesh, procreation does not occur.[3]

Even more remarkable is that the complementarity of wife and husband does not end with biology. In every dimension, physical, emotional, and intellectual, they fit like hand in glove; they match. The woman is better designed to nurture the child, to establish the family on the hearth, and to model how these things are done; the man is better designed to protect the mother and child, to establish the family in the world, and to model how those things are done. Even the virtues, though needed by both sexes, have male and female inflections. When escape is possible it is not an act of courage but rashness for an endangered woman to stay and fight, because she carries in herself the possibility of the next generation. But it is not an act of prudence but cowardice for the man to decline to defend her, because his life is only one. We may add that it is not an act of justice but of foolish injustice to pretend that the sexes are the same. Justice is exercised in respectfully providing for the due needs of each.

Spontaneous order. It may seem inconsistent to speak of spontaneous order as an aspect of species *design*: When we call order "spontaneous," don't we mean that it comes to pass without design? No, we mean that it comes to pass without superintendence. Design takes place beforehand; superintendence takes place afterward. Generally speaking, the achievement of spontaneous order requires more design, not less. If I toss nine three-inch-square blocks into a nine-inch-square box, then jostle the box, the blocks will spontaneously arrange themselves into a symmetrical three-by-three block grid. But they will do so only because they are just the right number, shape and size to fit, a set of features unlikely to arise by chance. In general, the more elaborate the spontaneous order, the more contrivance is necessarily to make it come to pass without supervision. "You can't get something out of nothing" applies not only to the matter and energy embodied in an arrangement, but to the information.[4]

The spontaneous order of the human species is that left to ourselves without supervision, we quickly form a rich array of associations such as families, neighborhoods, villages, businesses, vocational groups, religious societies, and schools. Edmund Burke wrote, "to be attached to the subdivision, to love the little platoon we belong to in society, is the first principle (the germ as it were) of public affections. It is the first link in the series by which we proceed toward a love to our country and to mankind. The interest of that portion of social arrangement is a trust in the hands of all those who compose it; and as none but bad men would justify it in abuse, none but traitors would barter it away for their own personal advantage."[5] Although the little platoons are varied and diverse, one of them is ubiquitous and fundamental: The family, based on the enduring conjugal partnership of the husband and wife. Indeed it seems to be the seed from which the others sprout. The first priests were the patriarchs of families; so were the first judges. The political community is not a primary association like the family, but a secondary association— an association of associations, a partnership of partnerships.

Because family is so sore beset and little honored in our day, it deserves special comment. No one invented it, no one is indifferent to it, and there was never a time in human history when it did not exist. Even when disordered, it persists. Members who are divided by disaster commonly undertake heroic efforts to reunite with each other. Only violence or strong ideology can abolish the family, and only small societies have even tried to abolish it; those which do try always fail, or else retreat gradually from their aims.

For the nurture of the young, the family has no parallel. In chapter two I quoted the remark of Sara S. McLanahan and Gary Sandefur that "If we were asked to design a system for making sure that children's basic needs were met, we would probably come up with something quite similar to the two-parent ideal." Of course—for it *is* designed, though not by us. And although it is not surprising that children, especially young ones, thrive less in orphanages than in the average family, it certainly ought to move us to awe that this is true even when care is taken to make the institutions homelike, and even when, in the eyes of sociologists, they are better organized than an average family *in every respect*— hygienically, medically, psychologically, and pedagogically.[6]

Nor has the extended family an equal for the moral development of adults. The old saw "You can choose your friends but you can't choose your relatives" captures one of the reasons: relatives are better moral training, just because we can't choose them. Chesterton explains it well:

In a large community we can choose our companions. In a small
community our companions are chosen for us. Thus in all exten-
sive and highly civilized societies groups come into existence
founded on what is called sympathy, and shut out the real world
more sharply than the gates of a monastery. There is nothing really narrow about the clan; the thing which is really narrow is the
clique. The men of the clan live together because they all wear the
same tartan or are all descended from the same sacred cow; but in
their souls, by the divine luck of things, there will always be more
colours than in any tartan. But the men of the clique live together
because they have the same kind of soul, and their narrowness is a
narrowness of spiritual coherence and contentment, like that which
exists in hell. . . . The best way that a man could test his readiness
to encounter the common variety of mankind would be to climb
down a chimney into any house at random, and get on as well as
possible with the people inside. And that is essentially what each
one of us did on the day that he was born.[7]

The other great reason is children. Offspring convert us; they force
us to become different beings. There is no way to prepare for them completely. They crash into our lives, they soil their diapers, they upset all
our comfortable arrangements, and nobody knows how they will turn
out. Willy-nilly, they knock us out of our complacent habits and force
us to live outside ourselves; they are the necessary and natural continu-
ation of that shock to our egotism which is initiated by marriage itself.
To receive this great blessing requires courage. But any so-called intimacy which is deliberately closed to new life eventually becomes a mere
collaboration in selfishness.

Subsidiarity. Culture should develop in partnership with our design, not
against it. It should function like a second nature, not fighting first nature, but filling the outline that first nature provides. This is usually called
the principle of connaturality. But from the individual and the family
at the base of the social order rise a hierarchy of associations, ascending

through neighborhoods, churches, vocational groups, and the other little platoons right on up to those institutions for public justice which we call government. The higher rungs are as necessary to the common good as the lower; however, the higher up the ladder we go, the less spontaneous their order, and the greater the need for contrivance. To put it another way, the higher the rung, the less help it gets from nature and the more help it needs from culture. We may call this the principle of diminishing spontaneity.

From these two principles together, we recognize a risk. The higher rungs *ought* to protect and cooperate with the more spontaneous lower rungs—but just because they *are* less spontaneous, they may not. The risk implies a rule. Higher rungs should be permitted to supply only those aspects of the common good which the lower rungs cannot. This, finally, is the principle of subsidiarity, which applies across the entire span of civil society: whether in the relation of family to neighborhood, union "local" to union federation, individual congregation to ecclesiastical communion, individual scholar to academic guild, voluntary association to government in general, or lower echelon of government to higher echelon.

Diminishing spontaneity and connaturality have been recognized by the natural law tradition since Aristotle. Oddly, although subsidiarity is a very plain corollary and was always implicit in the tradition, it came to the forefront only recently, acquiring its name from the Latin text of the following striking passage in a 1931 encyclical of the Roman Catholic pontiff, Pius XI:

> As history abundantly proves, it is true that on account of changed conditions many things which were done by small associations in former times cannot be done now save by large associations. Still, that most weighty principle, which cannot be set aside or changed, remains fixed and unshaken in social philosophy: Just as it is gravely wrong to take from individuals what they can accomplish by their own initiative and industry and give it to the community, so also

> it is an injustice and at the same time a grave evil and disturbance
> of right order to assign to a greater and higher association what
> lesser and subordinate organizations can do. For every social ac-
> tivity ought of its very nature to furnish help [*subsidium*] to the
> members of the body social, and never destroy and absorb them.[8]

As Pius explained, what pushed the principle of subsidiarity to the
forefront was the crisis in civil society brought about by the industrial
revolution. For a time it seemed as though the middle rungs of the ladder might be crippled or destroyed, leaving nothing but the vaunting
state at the top of the social scale and the solitary self at the bottom.
Collectivists and individualists made strange alliance to cheer this holocaust of the little platoons. The principle of subsidiarity reaffirms the
social design of the species, corrects both its individualist denial and its
collectivist perversion, and champions the rights and dignity of all of
those in-between associations which, if only allowed, will take root and
flourish, filling the valley between State and Self with fruit and color.

Having considered various aspects of our design, we must now consider what happens when we thwart them.

THE WITNESS OF NATURAL CONSEQUENCES

Thomas Aquinas describes law as a kind of discipline that compels
through fear of punishment.[9] He offers the comment in the context of
a discussion of human law, and so far as human law goes, I am sure his
meaning is clear. The human legislator attaches certain penalties to the
categories of acts he does not want done. For driving on the left side of
the road, I may be pulled over and made to pay a fine; for doing so frequently, I may be required to take a driving safety course; for continu-
ing to drive on the left side even then, I may forfeit my license; for driving
without a license, I may suffer the impoundment of my vehicle; and for
skidding around the corner and exceeding the speed limit to escape the

policeman, I may be sentenced to time in prison. Presumably this is the sort of thing that St. Thomas had in mind.

This trivial example illustrates three important points. First, the civil penalty is not the reason the act is wrong; if a man does not steal his neighbor's car only because he is afraid of serving time, we consider him base. The civil penalty *instructs* him that the act is wrong, and provides a further motive—if he needs one over and above the sheer wrong of it—for avoiding it. The *reason* the act is wrong is that it is contrary to the common good, and declared as such by public authority.

This declaration, by the way, not only announces what is needed for the common good but also to a certain degree "determines" it, and that is the second interesting thing about the example. After all, it is not *in itself* contrary to the common good to drive on the left side of the road. The thing which is contrary to the common good is for some to drive on the right, while others drive on the left. Just to insure that all drivers keep to the same side, the legislator commands that they drive on the right. Driving on the left thereby *becomes* contrary to the common good through his declaration, though it was not contrary to the common good before. He might have made it contrary to the common good to drive on the right, as in England, but he did not.

The third interesting thing about the example is that it reminds us that as a system of discipline, penalties are not perfectly efficient—nor is it likely that they could be, so long as people have free will. It is not just that people may seek to escape the penalties for wrongdoing; it is also that in order to escape them they may commit even greater wrongs and so become subject to even greater penalties. Remember the man driving without a license who skids around the corner and speeds to escape the policeman *so that* his car will not be impounded. Paradoxically, up to a certain degree of corruption in the will of the individual who is subject to the law, the civil penalty discourages violation—but beyond that point it stops discouraging and provides a motive to go further yet.

Let us leave the example for a moment and go back to Thomas Aquinas. I said he describes *law* as a kind of discipline that compels through fear of punishment. Although he offers the comment in the context of a discussion of human law, he seems to be speaking about law as such. Is his observation also true of the natural law? It is, and a great deal can be learned from this comparison. Just as there are civil penalties for breaking the human law, so there are natural penalties for breaking the natural law—and for those who don't read the road signs, they are one of the ways it is known. This too is a part of our design, but it is the way the design kicks back when we ignore it: the witness of natural consequences.

For breaking the foundational moral principles which we can't not know, one penalty is guilty knowledge, because deep down we can't help but know the truth. For breaking *any* precepts of the natural law, foundational or in the upper stories, there are other penalties too. Those who cut themselves bleed. Those who give offense to others are hated. Those who live by knives die by them. Those who betray all their friends have none left. Those who abandon their children have none to stroke their brows when they are old. Those who travel from bed to bed lose the capacity for trust. Those who torture their consciences are tortured by them in return. Those who suppress their moral knowledge become stupider than they had intended. Those who refuse the one in whose image they are made live as strangers to themselves. We see that the principle that God is not mocked, that whatever one sows he reaps,[10] is woven into the fabric of our nature. Not all our disobedience can unravel a single stitch. Some penalties show up within the lifetime of the individual; others may tarry until several generations have persisted in the same wrongdoing. But the penalties for defiance are cumulative, and eventually they can no longer be ignored.

We find a good example of such further penalties in the consequences of breaking the precept which confines sex to marriage.[11] An immediate consequence of their violation is injury to the procreative good: One might get pregnant but have nobody to help raise the child. Another immediate consequence is injury to the unitive good: One misses the chance for that total self-giving which can only develop in a secure and exclusive relationship. And there are long-term consequences too, among them poverty, because single women must provide for their children by themselves; adolescent violence, because male children grow up without a father's influence; venereal disease, because formerly rare infections spread rapidly through sexual contact; child abuse, because live-in boyfriends tend to resent their girlfriends' babies and girlfriends may resent babies which their boyfriends did not father; and abortion, because children are increasingly regarded as a burden rather than a joy. The longer people persist in violating the natural law, the heavier the penalties for violation. Provided they do not refuse the lesson, eventually even the dullest among us may put the clues together and solve the puzzle. Over the course of its history a culture may have to re-learn the timeless truths many times over. It may of course refuse to learn them and be destroyed.

At the outset I called attention to three interesting things about the civil penalties for violating human law. First, the penalty or consequence is not the reason the act is wrong; it only declares it's wrong and disciplines us for committing it. Second, the declaration of what is wrong not only announces what is needed for the common good; to a certain degree, it also "determines" it. Third, the system of penalties is not perfectly efficient; up to a certain degree of corruption in the will, the penalty discourages violation, but beyond that point it stops discouraging and actually provides a motive to go further yet. We may ask: Are all of these things also true about the *natural* penalties for violating *natural* law? The answer is "Yes." Let us see how.

1. *The consequence is not the reason the act is wrong; it only declares its wrong and disciplines us for committing it.* The way some parents and moralists harp about unwanted pregnancies and venereal disease, you would think

that if only condoms worked perfectly—if only they really could do away with unwanted pregnancies and venereal disease—then extramarital sex would be all right. What is wrong with this picture? Is it just that condoms *don't* work perfectly? No, for one could imagine a technology that did. Is it just that however perfect the technology, you couldn't get people to use it? No, for one can imagine an even better technology that worked independently of their wills. Then is it just that the list of bad consequences is incomplete—that even a perfect shield against pregnancy and disease would leave consequences like jealousy and mistrust untouched? No, for one can imagine a system of drugs and conditioning that would eliminate those consequences too, as in Huxley's *Brave New World.* What makes the people of Huxley's paradise so loathsome is that they don't understand the *point* of sex; they haven't a clue as to what it is for.

One should not be mistaken for a consequentialist just because he is willing to learn from consequences. "Good is to be done and pursued, and evil avoided" means more than "good ones are to be had and enjoyed, and evil ones to be got around." In fact, the most interesting point about the natural consequences of things is that they serve as a pointer to the natural purposes of things. The natural link between sex and pregnancy is not just a brute fact to be circumvented by latex; it declares that sex serves the purpose of procreation, of having and raising children in the love and fear of God. In the same way, the natural link between promiscuity and mistrust is not just an inconvenience to be sidestepped by lying; it declares that sex serves the related purpose of spousal intimacy, and should not be used to defeat it.

2. *The declaration of what is wrong not only announces what is needed for the common good, but also partly "determines" it.* We saw earlier that the common good is only partly given in advance of the human legislator's command. Driving on the left is not in itself contrary to the common

good, but becomes so when he has declared it so—just because then everyone else is driving on the right. He could have declared it contrary to the common good to drive on the right, and then it would have been contrary to the common good to drive on the right—because everyone else would be driving on the left. Whichever way he commanded, he would have assigned penalties accordingly. Of course this does not mean that he could have acted arbitrarily. The reason is that there is a deeper consideration which his command does not originate: We should not endanger our neighbors unnecessarily. That is why Thomas Aquinas says that even this sort of human law depends ultimately on natural law.[12]

In the same way that human law not only announces but partly determines the common good, so also the natural law not only announces but partly determines the common good. For God, we are told, acted freely in creation. He could have created a different universe than He did—a different nature, different in both final and efficient causalities—and then there would have been a different natural law, with different natural consequences for violation.

This does not mean that God's creation is arbitrary. The "determinations" of the human legislator find their boundary in the natural law; their originality is properly confined to pinning things down, or filling in the blanks. The only limit on God's creativity is His own Being, for God cannot act contrary to Himself; the only limit on the possible varieties of created goodness is His own, uncreated Goodness, of which we have no conception except by analogy with what He did create. For all we know he might have made three sexes rather than two, or arranged for us to procreate by budding rather than by bearing and begetting; but maybe not. For all we know he could have made the universe more different still, with other kinds of order *instead* of final and efficient causality; but maybe not. We don't know what might have been. We have no categories for thinking about it. The only categories available to us are the ones provided by the nature God *has* made, which is why it's so silly for people to speculate about things like whether He could have made a different moral order than he did. It's like a child asking, "If two and two made cheese, then what would monkeys equal?" All we know is that whatever God in His uncreated Goodness creates, is good.

I mention this only because it seems to be a real obstacle for contemporary people. We don't want the freedom of the creature but the freedom of the Creator—not freedom to be good but freedom to determine the good. Maybe this is not so new after all, for it was the first temptation: to be "like God, knowing good and evil." An honors student once asked me why sodomy *couldn't* promote the unitive good. I explained that different kinds of friendships have different natures and requirements; sexualizing a friendship does not necessarily help it come into its own. Although it consummates the friendship of wife and husband, it perverts the friendship of comrades, just as it perverts the friendship of parent and child. Then she wanted to know why sex *couldn't* consummate the friendship of two comrades. This time I explained that the difference between the spouses is crucial to the power of their union to take each out of Self for the Other. Sodomy resists that liberation; it is merely self-love with another body. Finally she wanted to know why sex *couldn't* take each comrade out of Self for the Other. And so finally I explained complementarity. A husband and wife can balance and complete each other, but the sexual reinforcement of identicals merely unhinges them; it makes them not less extreme, but more. The same dynamic of reinforcement takes place in the explosive promiscuity of men who mate men, and in the implosive dependency of women who mate women. That more or less satisfied her, but during the course of the conversation I realized that her problem was not just moral but also ontological. "You keep demanding 'Why *couldn't*,'" I suggested. "It's a little like demanding 'Why *couldn't* water run uphill, or the moon be made of green cheese.' I don't know how to make sense of the question. In this universe, it isn't, and this is the only one I know."

3. *The system of penalties is not perfectly efficient; up to a certain degree of corruption in the will of the person subject to the law, a penalty discourages violation, but beyond that point it actually provides a motive to go further.* The application to human law was that if a driver has a certain residue of good will, then the threat of losing his vehicle may keep him from driving without a license, but if he lacks even that residue, then he may drive at reckless speed just to keep the policeman from catching him. The penalty becomes a motive for further crime. This is one of the reasons, by the way, why human law should never be too far in advance of the level of virtue which the majority of the citizens have already achieved.[13]

Once again the analogy with natural law holds good. I suppose it is obvious how the point applies to the *physical* natural consequences of our acts. For instance consider pregnancy. You would think the fear of getting pregnant would deter unmarried people from playing around. Among those who retain a trace of chastity, it does. But those who lack that trace merely try to escape the natural consequence by trying to outrun the cop—that is, by using artificial contraceptives. When the contraceptives fail, some try even harder to escape the natural consequences by leaning out the window toward the approaching cop and firing at him with a gun—that is, by getting abortions. Count on it: if anyone invents a deintoxicating pill then drunkenness will increase; if anyone invents a perfect-memory pill there will be less knowledge in the world than before.

Less noticed, but even stronger, is how the point applies to the *noetic* natural consequences of our acts, to guilty knowledge. You would think that the terror of having to live with oneself afterward would deter people from getting abortions. Among some it does. But those who will not accept conscience as a teacher must face it as an accuser, and if they still run away they run into even deeper wrong. In this way, conscience urges them to yet further wrong. Consider the woman who told her counselor "I couldn't be a good parent," amended her remark to "I don't deserve to have any children," and still later revealingly added "If it hadn't been for my last abortion, I don't think I'd be pregnant now." We don't need a prophet to read the writing on this palace wall. When she says she couldn't be a good mother, what she means is that good mothers don't kill their children. She keeps getting pregnant to replace the children she has killed; but she keeps having abortions to punish herself for having killed them. With each abortion the cams of guilt make another revolution, setting her up to have another. She can never stop until she admits what is going on.

St. Thomas is right, then, when he describes law as a kind of discipline that compels, that drives us on, through fear of punishment: He is right about the human law, and yes, right about the natural law. But whether it compels us to obedience, or drives us on to further violation, depends on the condition of our hearts.

CLOSING CONSIDERATIONS

We are now in a position to sum up what we can't not know. Everyone knows inviolable goods like friendship, formal norms like fairness, and everyday moral rules like "Do not kill"—though we can pretend not to know them, and we sometimes err in what we derive from them. Everyone recognizes that the universe is designed and that we are designed —though we can refuse to pay attention, or pretend we haven't noticed. Everyone recognizes the most obvious features of our design, for example the complementarity of the sexes and the spontaneous order of the family—though the subtler features may take some reflection. Finally, everyone recognizes the most obvious inbuilt penalties of wrongdoing, for example that those who betray are not trusted—though not all these penalties are equally obvious, and if we are sufficiently obstinate they may provide a motive for further wrongdoing.

As we have seen, the four witnesses of deep conscience, design as such, our own design, and natural consequences have several features in common. In the first place, they all provide real moral knowledge. Of course, I have not proven that they do; I have only declared it. There is no way to prove the obvious. The time to demand proof is when a traveller claims he has visited a land where people have two heads, not when deep conscience says "You had better not cheat."

Another feature that all four witnesses have in common is that none of them provides *complete* moral knowledge. To fill in the details, experience and reflection are necessary.

The third is that in the final analysis *all four* witnesses presuppose design—even the first and the fourth. Unless conscience is designed, its voice is arbitrary and meaningless. Unless the natural consequences of our actions are designed, we may as well merely evade them (as many people try to do).

Theories of Natural Law as Theories of the Witnesses. The whole point of speaking of the four witnesses is to explain how it is that everyone knows something of the natural law, whether or not he has ever heard of any theories of it. Yet there is good reason to close this chapter with a few words about theories of natural law, just because they tend to share two weaknesses. One weakness is that most of them focus on this witness or that witness, virtually ignoring the other witnesses. More surprisingly, the design presupposition is often overlooked—not only by the people who study the theories, but sometimes by the theorists themselves.

Both weaknesses turn up in the theory of the early modern thinker Thomas Hobbes. Hobbes focuses exclusively on the witness of natural consequences—in fact, on just one natural consequence, death. We see this right away in his definition of a natural law as "a precept, or general rule, found out by reason, by which a man is forbidden to do that which is destructive of his life, or taketh away the means of preserving the same, and to omit that by which he thinketh it may be best preserved."[14] The narrowness of this view is breathtaking, but more amazing still is why he adopts it: He does so because he flatly denies the witness of our design. Hobbes insists that *no* inbuilt purposes and *no* ordering of goods can be discerned in human nature.[15]

Of course, this is nonsense. Hobbes plainly regards death as the greatest natural evil, our sole natural purpose merely to avoid it.[16] These points can hardly be sidestepped, for they are the basis of his whole theory. But if death is the greatest evil, then life is the greatest good, and there is an inbuilt ordering of goods after all. For all his efforts, then, all Hobbes did was substitute a narrow and impoverished view of our inbuilt purposes for the rich view embodied in the natural law tradition. Moreover his view is demonstrably false. As everyone knows, some things *are* worse than death.

A much more interesting and illuminating approach is the "new" natural law theory of John Finnis and Germain Grisez. Four years ago I would have accused it of the same two weaknesses that we find in the Hobbesian theory, for it too focuses on just one of the four witnesses, and it too seems to slight considerations of design. I now realize that this judgment was both uncharitable and imperceptive, for the picture is more complicated.[17]

The witness on which the Grisez and Finnis theory focuses is deep conscience, for their whole purpose is to try to show how the basic goods and the formal norms give rise to the everyday moral rules. It is true that they do not incorporate the testimony of the other three witnesses into their theory of natural law, and it is true that one of their reasons for not doing so is to avoid entangling the theory of conscience with the idea of inbuilt purposes. Nevertheless, it turns out that they do believe that we have been designed by God for certain purposes, they do agree about the features of our own design, and they do recognize the natural consequences of violating the natural law. They exclude these matters from their theory of deep conscience merely because they believe in them on other grounds. That can hardly be faulted; after all, the four witnesses are not the *same* witness, and witnesses two, three, and four are not contained in witness one. Thus, apart from certain technical differences which are hardly noticeable to non-specialists, it seems that the followers of Grisez and Finnis are largely in agreement with the tradition.

Besides this, they have made two great contributions to the tradition. The first is that they have given an impressive demonstration of just how many of the everyday moral rules can be derived from a few basic goods and formal norms. I am far from thinking that this is the route by which plain people know them, because some of these derivations are far from intuitive. Even so, the demonstration goes far toward showing why the four witnesses are in agreement, and it also sets a benchmark of logical rigor toward which the other schools of natural law thinking would do well to aim. The second contribution is that they have brought the inviolability and nonsubstitutability[18] of certain basic goods to the center of discussion. We may quarrel over some of these goods—I for one do not believe that what Grisez and Finnis call "the good of play" is inviolable and nonsubstitutable—but surely some goods are, for example innocent human life. Deliberately blowing up a schoolbus full of children is wrong no matter what might be gained by it, and it is no good to ask a grieving mother "Couldn't you just have another?" Emphasizing such facts has made it much easier than it used to be to explain just why theories like utilitarianism are so wrong.

The only point I would press here is that focusing on deep conscience does not really avoid entanglement with the idea of the inbuilt purposes of things, as the Grisez-Finnis theory supposes that it does. The idea of inbuilt purposes is implicit, for unless deep conscience has been designed to impart moral knowledge, there is no particular reason to think that it does impart moral knowledge: it is just a piece of driftwood, cast up on the shore of the human intellect by the eddies of natural selection—something like the way dogs scratch their ears with their hind legs. This, I think, is why those who sneer at the Grisez-Finnis theory also sneer for exactly the same reasons at other theories of natural law. To accept *any* witness is to accept design; to reject design is to reject every other witness.

A Final Point About Design. One more thought must be added before we go on to objections. Theories of natural law which focus on the second and third witnesses sometimes speak of "natural inclinations," and this has been badly misunderstood. A natural inclination is not whatever I happen to desire; it is not even whatever everyone desires. The point of the adjective "natural" is precisely to call attention to design. It is natural for me to be attracted to the opposite sex, even if I am actually attracted to my own. It is natural for me to eat a varied diet, even if I actually prefer eating nothing but chips and dip. It is natural for me to use my lungs to take in oxygen, even if I am actually addicted to sniffing glue. Our desires and tendencies do have significance when they are consequences of our design. But the mere fact that I want something or tend in a certain direction means nothing by itself, and the mere fact that all men do so means little more. On the contrary, if all of us want something in the teeth of our design, the reasonable inference is that something has gone wrong with us (a claim which my own faith considers literally true). So what matters is not how we "incline"—that may need correction. What matters is how we "naturally" incline—by the blueprint, by the layout, by the plan.

6

Some Objections

*Objections to these arguments can be
anticipated from various directions.*

ANYONE WHO CONSIDERS OBJECTIONS meets a dilemma. If he selects just a few, he disappoints those who say "You left mine out."
If he tries to reply to them all, he tries the patience of his readers. But if he eases the trial by dealing with them briefly, they wonder if
more should be said. In this chapter, I consider a fairly large number of
objections, but I deal with them conversationally, in the way I find they
actually arise. I have considered other objections in other ways in other
books.[1]

*You natural law thinkers seem to be confused about whether natural law
comes from God, from nature, from conscience, or from reason.*

There is no confusion, only a distinction. Traditionally, the authority of natural law has been found in the Creator, its content in the design He imparted to us, and the power by which we recognize it in the
faculty of reason—which is also a part of the design, and which includes
deep conscience as a part. In the older natural law terminology, the first

is called the "binding norm," the second the "discriminating norm," and the third the "manifesting norm."

Even so, to say that something is right just because it is natural is to commit the fallacy of deriving an "ought" from an "is."

No such fallacy has been committed. An "is" which merely "happens to be" has no moral significance because it is arbitrary; that's why it cannot imply an "ought." But an "is" which expresses the purposes of the Creator is fraught with an "ought" already. Such are the inbuilt features of our design, including the design of deep conscience.

I notice that you've already dropped the language of the three norms.

If it helps, I'll use it again. Put technically, your complaint confuses the discriminating norm with the binding norm. It treats nature as providing not only the content of the natural law but its authority. Natural law thinkers don't do that.

I'm still uncomfortable with this business about "nature" and the "natural." Didn't Aristotle and many others claim that even slavery was natural?

Yes, but they were wrong. It isn't.

Isn't that a bit glib?

Not at all. Slavery is about one being using another being merely as a means to its ends. A *what* may use a *what*, as a spider may eat a fly. A *who* may also use a *what*, as a man may eat a potato. But a *who* may not use a *who*—and human beings are *who*s. The fact that we are *who*s, not *what*s, is a feature of our design, and its significance is recognized by deep conscience, which is another feature of our design. Not even God merely uses us, because He would not dishonor His image.

Slavery was not my point. What I meant was that many grave moral wrongs have been committed in the name of natural law.

Of course. Evil has been done in the name of every good; lies have been propounded in the name of every truth. That is how sin works. Having nothing in itself by which to convince, on what other resources but good and truth can it draw to make itself attractive and plausible? We must use the natural law to recognize the abuse of the natural law; there is nothing else to use.

You still don't understand me. All sorts of wrongs are natural. It is natural to fly into a rage. It's natural to murder. Don't you get it?

You're mixing up two different senses of the word "natural." People *do* fly into rages and *do* murder, but the question is how we are designed. We are designed with a capacity for anger, to arouse us to the protection of endangered goods. It doesn't follow that anger should be indulged so far that goods are endangered. Aren't we also provided with brakes?

But we violate nature every time we have a cavity filled. Isn't it is natural for human beings to transcend their natures?

Saying that we violate the nature of a tooth every time we fill a cavity is like saying that we violate the nature of an automobile every time we plug a leak in the radiator. When we plug the leak, we are fulfilling the design by putting the car back in proper order. In the same way, filling a cavity restores to the tooth its natural function of chewing. Healing does not transcend our nature; it respects it.

So you would say that aspirin, surgery to remove a tumor, and cloning "respect" nature, too.

Not cloning.

Why not? Doesn't it assist the natural function of having babies?

Once more: Our nature is our design. We are designed to have babies, but we are not designed to have them *in that way*. To put it another way, our design includes not only certain ends but certain means. There is a difference between repairing the reproductive system and bypassing it.

Well, it doesn't seem to be a big deal anyway.

I think it is a very big deal. When you try to turn yourself into a different kind of being, you are not only doing wrong but asking for trouble. He who ignores the witness of his design will have to face the witness of natural consequences.

Why do you call anything the natural purpose of anything?

Why do we call steering the purpose of your car's steering wheel? Because in the first place it does steer the car, and in the second place that fact is part of the explanation of why the car has it.

Yes, but you're talking about human nature, not a car.

Why should the reasoning be different? New life is the chief purpose of our sexual powers, because in the first place they do cause new life, and in the second place that fact is part of the explanation of why *we* have them.

But you're assuming that our nature has a design just like a car has a design.

I'm not assuming anything; it's a reasonable conclusion from the evidence. A forensic pathologist *concludes* that the wounds on the victim's body were intended. An archaeologist *concludes* that the object he has dug up is an artifact. An intelligence analyst *concludes* that the radio blips he is picking up express a coded message. Watson *concludes* that the symbols cut into the bark of the tree were made by Holmes to point out the trail. In each case, the investigator infers that an intelligent agent has been at work because he has found a pattern which cannot be explained either by physical law, random chance, or law and chance together.[2]

But law and chance together do explain human nature. Darwin showed that. Random variation plus natural selection—remember?

We've been through this already. Darwin's theory fails Darwin's own test. Irreducible complexity—remember?[3]

Well, I'm not a specialist in biology. But that leads me to another problem. You say that natural law expresses the common moral sense of plain people, but plain people don't even understand these theories.

Saying that plain people don't know the natural law because they don't understand natural law *theory* is like saying that they don't know bodies fall because they don't understand the relativistic theory of gravitation. The phenomenon is one thing; the theory which describes and explains it is another.

So when you say plain people know the natural law, what exactly do you mean?

That there are moral basics they can't not know, like "Play fair," "Don't murder," and "Take care of your family." I don't mean that they know theoretical propositions like "There are moral basics we can't not know" or that they could explain to you about deep conscience and design inferences.

What good are the theoretical propositions, then?

They guard us from certain confusions, help out in a few difficult cases, and guide moral educators. And they help to answer people like you, who don't think folk *do* have real knowledge of the basics of right and wrong.

But you don't. There aren't any moral basics that everyone knows.

Of course there are. I just mentioned three of them: "Play fair," "Don't murder," and "Take care of your family."

Those are just platitudes. Everyone has his own idea of "playing fair."

Does he? Try making up your own idea of what's fair—say, "giving the greatest rewards to the laziest workers"—and see how seriously people take you.

But some people don't play fair.

I haven't argued that people always obey these precepts. I've only argued that they know them.

If they don't always obey them, how do you know that they know them?

Because even when they don't obey them, they betray the telltale signs of guilty knowledge. For example, they make excuses. They try to convince everyone that they *are* playing fair and the *others* aren't.

But if there are things we "can't not know," then how is it even possible to make excuses?

People make excuses by *using* what they can't not know. All folk know that you ought to return a favor, so to rationalize not returning one they pretend either that they did return it or that it wasn't a favor. All folk know the wrong of deliberately taking innocent human life, so in order to rationalize murder they play games with the meaning of "wrong," "deliberate," "taking," "innocent," "human," or "life." Excuses are not evidence that people don't know the natural law, but that they do.

What about people who really don't know what they "can't not know?"

How do you know they don't know it?

Because they say they don't.

Like relativists, thieves, and abortionists?

Well, yes.

I don't believe them.

So when someone denies that he knows the natural law, your only answer is "That just proves you're in denial."

Not at all. Everyone knows that it's wrong to cheat. If someone tells me that he has no such knowledge, it's true that I don't believe him. But I don't confuse denying it with "being in denial." For evidence that he really is in denial, I look elsewhere. For example, see how quickly he complains of injustice when someone tries to cheat *him*.

Here's someone who doesn't know what he "can't not know": the cannibal. He doesn't know that he shouldn't murder.

It is most unlikely that he doesn't know the wrong of deliberately taking innocent human life. What is much more likely is that he doesn't think the people in the other tribe are human.

What good is it to honor human life if you don't know who is human?

I didn't say he doesn't *know* that the people in the other tribe are human. I said he doesn't *think* that they are. Deep down, even the cannibal knows better. Otherwise, why does he perform elaborate expiatory rituals before he takes their lives?

Suppose you're right, and people do know the moral basics. Then why is it necessary to remind them?

We touched on that a few minutes ago. Are you asking why moral education is necessary?

Yes. If we already know what moral education has to tell us, then what purpose does it serve?

Moral education serves at least five purposes. It reinforces what we know, because the mere fact that we know something is wrong is not enough to keep us from doing it. It elicits what we know, because we know many things without noticing that we know them. It guards what we know, because although deep conscience cannot err, surface conscience can err in all too many ways. It builds upon what we know, because only the most general and basic matters of right and wrong are known to us immediately, and second knowledge must be added to first. Finally, it confronts us about what we know, because sometimes we need to be told "You know better."

You speak of what we already know, but surely children don't already know the natural law.

Correct. When we speak of things we can't not know we have in mind people who have reached the age of reason. That's why I've sometimes described the natural law as what we can't not know "or can't help learning." Although I suspect that even children know more than you think. When Billy steals Susan's cupcake, Susan knows enough to cry "Not fair!", and Billy knows enough to lie about it.

You mean so that he won't be spanked.

Right.

But doesn't that show he doesn't know he did wrong?

No. It shows that violating one known duty gives Billy an immediate motive to violate another.

So you think even pretty young children know some of the natural law.

Yes. Some of it.

But not all of it.

Not all.

But if children don't know all of it, it isn't innate knowledge after all.

Who said it was?

Don't all natural law thinkers say it is?

No. That's a common misconception. When you say "innate," you mean something like "born with us." How could the newborn baby know that gratuitously hurting people is wrong, when he doesn't even know that there are people?

But if the so-called first principles aren't innate, then how can you call them "first"?

They aren't first in the order of time, but in the order of presuppositions. They are the unprovables from which proofs are built. The reason it takes a long time to know things like "Gratuitously hurting people is wrong" is that it takes a long time to form concepts of gratuitousness, hurting, people, and wrong. Our minds are so designed that as soon as we do grasp these concepts, we immediately recognize that gratuitously hurting people is wrong. The technical expression is that the precept, though not innate, is *per se nota*, "known in itself," "underived."

I don't buy that. If everyone knows certain precepts, it's only because everyone is taught them.

In that case it's mighty strange that everyone is taught the same precepts. How do you explain the fact that the same ones are taught everywhere?

The same ones aren't taught everywhere. Christians restrict a man to one wife; Muslims permit up to four.

We were talking about basics, not details. Show me a society that doesn't recognize the institution of marriage!

But that's only for the preservation of the species.

I thought you were trying to tell me that there isn't any natural law. Now you're trying to tell me why there is.

No, what I mean is that I concede the reality of instincts. All this talk of "conscience" is just mystification.

Morality is not an instinct. If it were, we might *think* we should resist it, but we wouldn't be able to. The facts are just the opposite. We *can and do* resist it, but think we shouldn't.

So maybe it's not an instinct; call it a predisposition, or just prudence. It's still about preservation. We want our kind to survive. Sometimes what is needed for survival goes against my personal wishes, that's all.

Who do you mean by "our kind"? What helps a family to survive might not help the larger society to survive. What helps society to survive might not help a particular family to survive.

I mean our species. I'm talking about the human race.

That's a little arbitrary, isn't it? Don't people want their families and their societies to survive too? Besides, morality is not about whether the human race survives, but about what kind of survival it gets. We marry;

guppies don't. We don't eat our young; they do. Yet neither species is in danger of extinction.

But all this talk about "conscience" is rot. Moral beliefs are pumped in from outside. Some people never acquire any at all.

You mean the famous "people without a conscience." But we've been through this before too.[4] There is a difference between guilty knowledge and guilty feelings. Not everyone feels guilty for murder, but everyone knows murder is wrong. Precisely because they have guilty knowledge, wrongdoers who lack guilty feelings show other telltales, such as depression, a sense of defect, a compulsion to rationalize,[5] or a puzzling desire to be caught. The suicide rate among sociopaths is also higher than in the general population.

So maybe we do all have conscience. But I still think it's pumped in from outside. If I want to teach Billy that hurting people is wrong, I just say "Billy, don't hurt people. It's wrong."

That's a very good thing to tell him, and I strongly recommend it. But what do you say when he asks "Why is it wrong?"

I say "It just is."

So do I, but that's just my point. The reason you can draw that fact to Billy's attention is that once his attention is drawn to it, he can see it for himself. But suppose he didn't. Suppose he didn't even know the meaning of wrong. What would you do then?

I'd tell him "Wrong is what you ought not do."

By itself that would teach him only that "wrong" and "what you ought not do" mean the same thing. It wouldn't teach him *what* same thing they meant. If he already knows what "ought not" means, then you've given him a synonym. If he doesn't know what "ought not" means, then he doesn't know what "wrong" means either.

In that case I'll tell him "Wrong is what you'll be punished for."

Come now, you don't believe that yourself. Generally speaking, wrong should be punished. But if a wrong goes unpunished, does that mean it isn't wrong after all?

Point taken. I'll teach him "Wrong is what you ought *to be punished for."*

Then you've merely led him in a circle: Wrong is what it would be wrong *not* to punish him for. You've explained wrong in terms of wrong. The explanation presupposes the thing you are trying to explain.

Then how do you teach him what wrong means?

We can teach first principles in a sense, but we don't "pump them in." The mind is so designed as to acquire them on its own, as the eye is designed to see on its own. What we call teaching only helps the process along. When we instruct and discipline the child we are only calling his attention to the first principles, giving him words for them, building on them, extending them, and reinforcing them with praise and punishment. Billy learns the meaning of the word "red" because whenever something is red, I say "red." He learns the meaning of the word "same" because whenever two things are the same, I say "same." And he learns the meaning of the word "wrong" because whenever something is wrong, I say "wrong." But a child without the rudiments of *synderesis* could not be taught the meaning of the word "wrong" for the same reason that a child without sight could not be taught the meaning of the word "red" and a child without the power of comparison could not be taught the meaning of the word "same." The child has to be able to see for himself what I am drawing to his attention.

Maybe we make up right and wrong. Maybe human nature doesn't have any inbuilt meaning; maybe the way of life I choose has moral meaning just because I choose it.

If you say that, aren't you supposing that one part of human nature does have meaning apart from your choosing—the will, the choosing power itself?

Why do you say that?

Because if it didn't *have* meaning, then how could it *give* it? You can't get something from nothing; you can't get meaning from the meaningless. When you say that human nature has no inbuilt meaning so that only your choices matter, what you're really saying is that exactly one part of human nature does have inbuilt meaning: The part that makes your choices.

What difference does that make?

It's a bit arbitrary, isn't it? If the will has inbuilt meaning, why shouldn't the other parts of human nature have inbuilt meaning too? Why should every part be meaningless except that one?

So what if they do have moral meaning? That doesn't stop the will from having moral meaning.

Of course not. But it stops it from having the meaning that you want it to. It isn't free to *confer* meanings on things that have inbuilt meanings already.

In that case, maybe nothing has moral meaning.

If you really believed that were true, then you wouldn't bother to argue with me.

Then maybe we create moral meaning.

Even supposing that human beings can create, surely a morality is not the *kind* of thing we can create. The whole meaning of morality is a norm which obligates us whether we like it or not. If we create it, then we can change it to suit ourselves. But if we can change it to suit ourselves, then it is not morality.

But we create other things. Why not this one?

I think I've just told you why not! But in fact we cannot genuinely create anything; we are inventive, but our inventiveness is not of that kind.

Why isn't it?

Because to create is to bring something forth from nothing. We humans can bring forth only from materials that are already available. We can bend the *givens* of human nature this way or that, but we cannot give ourselves new *givens*. Even if we could give ourselves new *givens,* the choice of which *givens* to give ourselves would be conditioned by what had been given before. To put this another way, if you ask a human being "What would you wish to become, if you could become anything you wished?", then his answer will be conditioned by the fact that he is *now* a human being. He may ask to have nonhuman attributes—like the ability to fly—but he will never ask to have attributes that a *human being* finds unattractive. I suppose you know the story about Friedrich Nietzsche and the dust of the earth.

And the dust of the earth? No. Tell it to me.

Nietzsche says to God, "I too can create a man." God says to Nietzsche, "Try." Nietzsche takes a fistful of dust and begins to mold it. God says, "Disqualified. Get your own dust."

I don't see the point.

It's just what I was saying. We can't really create. That's why, as C.S. Lewis explained,[6] the so-called new moralities are never new. All they ever do is distort something they have borrowed from the old morality.

What do you mean by the "old" morality? Conventional mores?

Not exactly. The natural law.

Give me an example of a new one.

We've already had one—your new morality of will. A person's choices certainly deserve some respect. But you blew this up into the principle that a person's choices deserve *absolute* respect. In its name you denied every other moral consideration whatsoever.

I'm still not convinced that I was wrong. Give me another example.

Certainly. The old morality commands compassion and prohibits murder. The new morality of euthanasia justifies murder *in the name* of "compassion"—a bogus compassion which doesn't care how the painful sight is made to go away. Just as in the other case, a single precept is first distorted, then wielded against the rest of moral law.

So you think these new moralities fob off picking and choosing as creating.

Exactly. They don't make something from nothing; they choose and pervert an element of what is already there.

But human beings do create morality. What do you call culture?

Culture doesn't create new frameworks of moral possibility. It discovers, elaborates, and make choices among possibilities within a framework already given. Or—if it goes bad—then it fights that framework, but even then it does not create a new one.

I don't like the sound of this. If there really is a natural moral law, then democracy is over with.

Why?

Because there would be no decisions left for legislators to make. If they did try to make any, judges would just say "The natural law says" and overrule them.

That's doubly mistaken. In the first place, there would be plenty of decisions left for legislators to make.

Why?

Because only the foundational principles of the natural law are known to all—only the moral basics. The remote implications remain to be worked out and fashioned into rules.

But if judges thought the legislators had worked out those remote implications badly, they would invoke natural law to overrule them.

Some might try. But there is only one situation in which it would be allowable for courts to refuse to recognize a legislative act on grounds of natural law—if the legislature had violated one of the moral basics, for example by authorizing some people to murder others. The reason judges could invoke the natural law against legislators in *that* sort of case is that they know the moral basics every bit as well as legislators do. But here's the rub: Judges are *not* just as good at working out the remote implications of the natural law. They have no call to refuse to recognize a legislative act in that sort of matter—much less make law on their own.

Why aren't they just as good at working out the remote implications of the natural law?

Because of the difference in their job. Legislative procedures are adapted to developing general rules; judicial procedures are adapted to applying these general rules to the facts of particular cases. Courts do not anticipate cases not actually before them; legislatures *must* anticipate cases not actually before them. That is what we have them for.

So you're saying that nothing in the natural law forbids the separation of functions.

That's right. It's perfectly all right for the framers of a constitution to give one job to legislatures and a different job to courts. I think they should, myself.

So it's okay for legislatures to consider the natural law, but not okay for courts to do so.

That's not how I'd put it.

Sorry; I should have said, so it's okay for both courts and legislatures to consider the moral basics—but only legislatures should consider their remote implications.

That's not quite how I'd put it either.

How would you put it, then?

It's okay for both courts and legislatures to consider the moral basics—but as to their remote implications, courts should *defer* to legislatures.

Isn't that what I said?

No. There is a difference between not considering the remote implications at all, and deferring to the legislature about them.

I don't see why.

How about an example? Here's how one codification of law explains when contracts are binding and when they aren't: "A promise which the promisor should reasonably expect to induce action or forbearance of a definite and substantial character on the part of the promisee and which does induce such action or forbearance is binding if injustice can be avoided only by enforcement of the promise."[7]

Put more simply, if breaking the promise would cause injustice, then the contract is binding.

Correct. Now suppose that the legislature has enacted that wording into law, and a court has to interpret it. Do you see a problem?

No.

The legislature hasn't told the court what injustice is. It expects the court to know that already.

Oh, yes. But so what?

So even though the court defers to the legislature by accepting the general rule which the legislature has given to it, it may be forced to work out *some* of the remote implications of the natural law, just to figure out what the legislature means. But it still accepts legislative intent as the rule.

I see now.

Then you see that nothing about the natural law encourages judges to lose their heads.

Perhaps not.

I would even say that the strongest encouragement to runaway judicial activism is *denying* the natural law.

So you say. But I still don't like the sound of this. Maybe natural law doesn't spell the end of democracy, but surely it spells the end of tolerance.

What do you mean?

Just what I said. If there really is a natural moral law, then tolerance goes out the window.

You think everyone ought to be tolerant, is that it?

Yes. And so do you—or you ought to. And you know it.

I do. But consider. You've just said that the duty of tolerance is both right for all, and known, or at least knowable, to all. But to say that is to call it a natural law.

Trivially, yes. But for all I know, it's the only one.

It can't be the only one. Consider again. You don't think we should tolerate everything, do you?

No, I suppose not.

But without the rest of morality, how do you know what should be tolerated and what shouldn't be?

But if we should only tolerate what is morally right, then the virtue of tolerance is redundant.

I didn't say we should tolerate only what's morally right.

Pardon me, but you did. You said that the measure of what should be tolerated is the moral law.

That's doesn't mean we should tolerate only what's morally right. Some moral wrongs must be tolerated because suppressing them would require further moral wrongs. Wrong does not become right just because it is committed to prevent a wrong.

Give me an example.

Here is an old, old example from the days when the Christian faith was supported by the state. No parents, it was argued, should refuse to let their children be baptized. The question arose whether the children of obstinate parents should be baptized against their parents' wills. The answer was no. Doing so would violate the natural authority of parents to teach their children, which is itself ordained by God in the natural law. The wrong of parental obstinacy was tolerated because suppressing it would require moral wrong on the part of official busybodies.

You're insufferable. Even your tolerance is moralistic.

In a sense, certainly. But you are a moralist, too. You became one the moment you said that one *ought* to practice tolerance.

But the other party may disagree with your morality.

Of course, but I can't help that. Any way of deciding what to tolerate is *some* way of deciding what to tolerate. The other party may disagree with yours.

No. Tolerance requires being fair to both moral views.

What if the two sides have different views of fairness? To be fair to different views of fairness you have to implement *some* view of fairness.

No. Fairness requires moral neutrality.

What do you mean by moral neutrality?

I mean suspending moral judgment.

If you really suspended moral judgment, you couldn't judge what to tolerate. You couldn't even judge *whether* to tolerate. Tolerance requires practicing moral judgment, not suspending it.

I don't mean suspending moral judgment. I mean giving equal standing to every moral point of view.

That merely gives higher standing to the opinion that morals are relative to point of view.

I don't mean giving equal standing to every moral point of view. I mean seeking moral common ground.

I believe in the moral common ground too, but there is only one moral common ground, and that is the natural law itself—common by virtue of our shared human nature. What you mean by common ground is something different. You want a way of making a decision without taking sides. That's impossible.

Of course it's possible. The tolerant solution to the abortion controversy, for example, is that the state should refuse to take sides, letting people make up their own minds.

What you call letting people make up their own minds about the issue *is* taking sides on the issue. You are siding with those who want the killing to be permitted, against those who want it to be forbidden.

But I'm neither pro-abortion nor anti-abortion. I'm pro-choice.

The cause of legalized abortion is no more "pro-choice" than the cause of legalized slavery. Although it facilitates certain choices, it makes others impossible. To "choose" to abort the child is to deny him the choice to live, and to "choose" to legalize killing him is to deny his defenders the choice to protect him by law. The issue is not whether to allow a choice, but which choices to allow.

I still think your approach is authoritarian.

The only thing authoritarian in these debates is your so-called neutrality.

How could neutrality be authoritarian?

It is authoritarian because it is a facade. Neutralism is a method of ramming a particular moral judgment into law by pretending that it is not a moral judgment.

Still, it bothers me that natural law theory is so religious. You talk about God "ordaining" the natural law.

Funny that you should say that. All too often natural law thinkers are accused of not being religious *enough*.

Why?

Some Christians—a minority, but a majority in some circles—say that the only place to find moral truth is in the word of God, and that natural law tradition denies this. They argue that the natural law tradition puts much too much confidence in the capacity of fallen man to know the moral truth. They worry that the first people to use the expression "natural law" were the Stoics, who were pagans. Finally, they suspect that the God of natural law is not the God of the Bible, but the God of Deism—a distant Creator who designed the universe, wound it up, set it running, then went away.

If I were a Christian, I might find those arguments plausible myself. How do you answer them?

Where do you want me to start?

With the first one. Since you're a Christian, why not just rely on the Bible?

For several reasons, but the best one is that the Bible itself testifies to the reality of the natural law.

Does it actually mention natural law?

It doesn't use the term "natural law," but it alludes to all four witnesses.[8] For example, St. Paul mentions the witness of deep conscience when he writes, "When Gentiles who have not the law [of Moses] do by nature what the law requires, . . . [t]hey show that what the law requires is written on their hearts, while their conscience also bears witness and their conflicting thoughts accuse or perhaps excuse them."[9] He captures the discipline of natural consequences in the formula, "Do not be deceived; God is not mocked, for whatever a man sows, that he will also reap."[10] The Bible is big on the witness of design—design in general, design in us. And it's remarkable that when the apostles are speaking to pagans, they don't begin with scripture, but with what the pagans know already—for instance their longing for an "unknown god," which implies knowledge that none of their deities are adequate.[11]

Comment on the second criticism—how did you put it?—that natural law thinkers put too much confidence in the capacity of fallen man to know moral truth.

In his letter to the Christians in Rome, St. Paul doesn't blame the pagans for not having the truth about God and His moral requirements, but for suppressing and neglecting it.[12] In the Proverbs, the complaint made about "fools" is not primarily that they lack knowledge but that they despise it.[13] In other words, atheism and moral obtuseness are not primarily an intellectual flaw; their most important ingredient is obstinacy. The natural law tradition does not deny these things. It recognizes error, it recognizes obstinacy, and it recognizes self-deception. As you may remember, that's why it distinguishes *synderesis* from *conscientia*.

What about the third criticism, that natural law is just a baptized pagan theory?

It's true that the first philosophers to use the *term* "natural law" were pagans, but the biblical testimony to its reality came earlier still. Besides, if God *has* made some things plain through the four witnesses, wouldn't you expect the pagan philosophers to notice them? Of course their theories needed correction at many points, but that has been done.

If they were talking about the things we "can't not know," then why would they need correction?

We've been over this several times. The moral basics are one thing; the best way to describe them is another. It's the former that we can't not know. Getting the latter right has taken centuries. The work is far from done; and our stubborn wills resist its completion.

Sorry. The fourth criticism, then—that the God of natural law is different from the God of Scripture.

No, it's an incomplete picture of the same one. Nature proclaims its Creator; Scripture tells you who He is. Nature shows you the results of His deeds in creation; Scripture tells you the results of His deeds in history. Nature manifests to you His moral requirements; Scripture tells you what to do about the fact that you don't measure up to them. Scripture is more important because it tells you the plan of salvation, but not even Scripture makes nature superfluous. It presupposes that you know the four witnesses already.

Well, this little digression about Christianity has been interesting, but it only strengthens my feeling that natural law theory is too religious.

What do you mean by "too religious"?

You only say there is a God because of the Bible.

I say there is a God because His reality is by far the best explanation of a great many features of our existence. Including the fact that we exist. The Bible agrees, but it would be true even if there were no Bible.

Be that as it may, morality stems from human need and interest.[13]

Is this what you mean? We are so made that we need to love God; we are so made that we need to love our neighbors; we are so made that we need to develop the virtues. Also, we are so made as to be interested in truth; we are so made as to be receptive to the demands of friendship; we are so made as to be attracted, despite ourselves, to moral goodness. These are what *I* call human need and interest—the needs and interests which arise from the design of human nature.

No, that's not what I mean.

Then what do you mean?

I'm not sure, but not that.

Could it be that you want man to be to himself what God has been to man hitherto?

What if I do? What would be wrong with that?

I see three problems with it, all very practical. The first problem is that if man is to assume the office of God to himself, he will have to square it with the present occupant. I think he may find that difficult.

Not if there is no God.

That's a mighty big counterfactual. But the second problem is that you're too late. Man has already been created. He has already been provided with being. It is too late for him to give himself a different being than he has.

But it's not too late to change it.

To monkey with it, you mean. The third problem is that when you say "man," you mean *some* men.

Why?

You say you want man to be to himself what God has been to man. But what God has been to man is man's absolute superior, and man cannot be his own superior. A thing can be equal to itself, but it cannot be greater than itself. So when you say you want man to be to himself what God has been to man hitherto, you mean you want some men to be to *other* men what God has been to man. You want some men to be the absolute superiors of others. I assume that you want to be in the former group and not in the latter. And so when you say morality stems from human need and interest, you mean you want it to stem from *your* needs and interests, over against the needs and interests of the others.

That's not what I mean at all.

Forgive me, but it is exactly what you mean. You say you want to change the human design. But in that case there must be two groups: Those who cause the change, and those who result from it. And the former hold all the cards.

The future men will thank us for it.

If you have changed them, will they be men?

PART III

HOW IT WAS LOST

*It seems strange that what we can't not know
could be forgotten; yet, in a sense, it has been.*

— 7 —

Denial

There is nothing wrong with the basic programming of conscience; the problem is in the interface, the human will.

DESPITE THE IMPORTANCE OF CONSCIENCE, I have so far treated it in less detail than the other three witnesses. There is a reason; conscience presents paradoxes which the other three witnesses do not. Deep conscience cannot err, but in working out its remote implications we can err, so that surface conscience becomes misleading. More troubling than erring, we can lie, telling ourselves that we don't know what we do. Lies and errors compound each other so that the opening between what we know and what we believe gapes like a wound in a body. From ancient times a conscience in such condition has been called "seared"[1]: The depth is red and bloody, but the surface is dry and tough.

THE FIVE FURIES

Though I have alluded to the paradoxes of conscience in the previous chapters, we have come to the point where we must consider them in more detail, and there is matter here for dread.

Everyone knows that conscience works in two different modes. In the cautionary mode, it alerts us to the peril of moral wrong and generates an inhibition against committing it. In the accusatory mode, it indicts us for wrong we have already done. The most obvious way of doing so is through the feeling of remorse, but remorse is the least of the Furies. No one always feels remorse for doing wrong; some people never do. Yet even when remorse is absent, guilty knowledge generates objective needs for confession, atonement, reconciliation, and justification. These other Furies are the greater sisters of remorse: inflexible, inexorable, and relentless, demanding satisfaction even when mere feelings are suppressed, fade away, or never come. And so it is that conscience operates not only in the first two modes but in a harrowing third: The avenger, which punishes the soul who does wrong but who refuses to read the indictment.

Conscience is therefore teacher, judge, or executioner, depending on the mode in which it works: cautionary, accusatory, or avenging.

How the avenging mode works is not difficult to grasp. The normal outlet of remorse is to flee from wrong; of the need for confession, to admit what one has done; of atonement, to pay the debt; of reconciliation, to restore the bonds one has broken; and of justification, to get back in the right. But if the Furies are denied their payment in wonted coin, they exact it in whatever coin comes nearest, driving the wrongdoer's life yet further out of kilter. We flee not from wrong, but from thinking about it. We compulsively confess every detail of our story, except the moral. We punish ourselves again and again, offering every sacrifice except the one demanded. We simulate the restoration of broken intimacy, by seeking companions as guilty as ourselves. And we seek not to become just, but to justify ourselves.

All of the Furies collude. Each reinforces the others, not only in the individual but in the social group. Perhaps you and I connive in displaced reconciliation by becoming comrades in guilty deeds. Or perhaps my compulsion to confess feeds your compulsion to justify yourself. In such ways entire groups, entire societies may drive themselves downhill, as the revenge of conscience grows more and more terrible.

My examples focus on abortion, which is both the chief means by which our own society is losing moral sanity and the greatest symptom of its loss. The discussion has been seasoned with other illustrations just to show how broadly the Furies do their work.

THE FIRST FURY: REMORSE

Remorse may fade, but it may also grow. In some people it increases gradually, with age and maturity; something which did not bother me much in thoughtless youth may bother me a great deal when I have had more experience of life. In some it lies fallow for a while, then suddenly appears. I thought I had left it behind, but I had not; it enters my mind all at once, massive, raw, unbidden, demanding service. The reappearance may be periodic—say on the anniversary of the deed. Or it may be occasional, when I come across things that remind me of it. A birth announcement. A letter from my parents. A scent of perfume, or of antiseptic.

But the most dreadful way remorse grows is by repetition of the deed, and the bitter fact is that although our efforts to dull the ache by not thinking about it may work after their fashion, they also make repetition more likely.

The simplest example comes from a recovering alcoholic who said to me that he knew exactly what I meant: "A drunk is ashamed of being a drunk—so he gets drunk."

Needless to say, there are many other ways to keep from thinking, some of them stone-cold sober.

One way is to set up a diversion. Because I refuse to give up my real transgressions, I invest other things with inflated significance and give up those things instead. Perhaps I have pressured three girlfriends into abortion, but I oppose war and capital punishment, I don't wear fur, and

I beat my chest with shame whenever I slip and eat red meat. Easier to face invented guilt than the thing itself.

I might also be able to keep from thinking about my deeds by averting my eyes from their consequences—for example by making someone else deal with them. Mary Meehan writes,

> Early abortions can be done by suction machines because the fetal bones and cartilage have not yet hardened. In the very earliest stages, this results in pureed remains. Even a little later, though, it brings out identifiable body parts that must be reassembled to ensure that nothing was left behind. . . . Dr. Beverly McMillan used to do such reassembly after performing abortions, but "I got to where I just couldn't look at the little bodies any more." Many abortionists do not reassemble the parts themselves, but have other staff do it. Some staffers are not bothered by this; indeed, some are hardened enough to make jokes about it. Others do not want anything to do with it. "Clinic workers may say they support a woman's right to choose," said former Planned Parenthood clinic worker Judith Fetrow, "but they will also say that they do not want to see tiny hands and feet."[2]

Another common way not to face what I am doing is to pretend I am doing something else. A study of the U.S. clinical trials of the "abortion pill" RU486, or mifepristone/misoprestol, found that some women preferred it to surgical abortion just because it lent itself to such denial.

Rochelle: With the pill, it was more *natural*, something more natural, [than] sticking something in me.

Wendy [interviewer]: What do you mean by more natural?

Rochelle: It felt like going through my period, so it felt like a natural process.

As the authors remark, "considering the abortion to be just like bad menstrual cramps may be a way of conceptualizing the process as not-really-abortion, but rather, as the late period that finally comes."[3] Staff who administered the drug for the trials thought so too. As a surgical services assistant put it, "I think they were pretty much in denial as to the fact that they were having an abortion and most of them were, I found, patients who wouldn't even say 'abortion.' I think they denied it." A midwife-nurse practitioner said much the same thing: "I think for some women, there was a connection between more natural, more like a miscarriage. A miscarriage is okay; an abortion is not okay. So if I'm having a miscarriage I can tell everybody I had a miscarriage. I didn't pay for someone to put an instrument in my uterus and remove my pregnancy." Plainly this woman was in denial herself: she called abortion "removing a pregnancy," though she knew quite well what it removes.

Some staff were resentful that the women tried to think of their abortions as miscarriages. Others played along, considering the self-deception good. Remarked one physician, "I think there are people who want to be in denial about whether it's really an abortion or not. I think that's fine. . . . For some people that's a very useful denial and more power to them if they have to use that not to have an unwanted child." The authors, who are strongly pro-abortion, seem to agree: "Indeed, denial may be considered a form of agency, in that it enables women who are troubled about abortion to get through the experience more easily."[4] The presupposition here is that remorse over abortion is merely a symptom of disordered thinking. Whenever it surfaces, they intone that the stricken women "appeared to have been influenced by anti-abortion rhetoric" or "may also have been influenced by anti-abortionists' claims." Their only regret about the miscarriage euphemism is that it doesn't work for conventional abortion, which clients inconveniently call "ripping the baby apart." As the authors lament, "there is no available pro-choice language for talking about the nitty-gritty of abortion itself."[5]

Not that its advocates haven't tried to find one. The famous Colorado abortionist Warren M. Hern, author of a textbook on abortion practice, says in an article that human pregnancy "may be defined as an illness" which "may be treated by evacuation of the uterine contents" and "has an excellent prognosis for complete, spontaneous recovery if managed under careful medical supervision."[6]

Except for the opening example I have focussed on the sober ways of displacing remorse, but drug and alcohol abuse are common ways too, and not just among alcoholics. Their proportions among abortion staff are legendary. Nita Whitten, a former abortion secretary to an abortion facility in Texas, explains: "I took drugs to wake up in the morning. I took speed while I was at work. And I smoked marijuana, drank lots of alcohol. . . . this is the way that I coped with what I did. It was horrible to work there, and there was no good in it." Unfortunately, refusing to think about the horror of abortion did not serve her well; later she had an abortion herself, fell into depression, and at one point became suicidal. Abhorrence of what one is doing sinks in even if it does not register consciously. Kathy Sparks, a former assistant in an Illinois abortion facility, remarks that the first time she witnessed an abortion she considered it no different than the dissection of a frog in biology class. Yet like other staffers at her center, she too started drinking heavily and using drugs.[7]

The usefulness of alcohol as an instrument of avenging remorse also helps explain a variety of other social phenomena, for example the popularity of so-called singles bars as places for the sexes to meet. One would hardly expect it, because "hooking up" is emotionally difficult for young women: what they want is a bond of commitment.[8] To be sure, it damages the capacity to make bonds in young men too, but at a certain age men may imagine that they don't need them—a fantasy women find implausible at any age. Many young women drink before meeting new men just so that if sexual intercourse follows, they will be able to go through with it. Unfortunately, drinking also makes intercourse more likely to follow, so they feel emptier still, and the next time the need for alcohol is even greater.

THE SECOND FURY: CONFESSION

Deflected from repentance, the confessional need seeks satisfaction in various oblique ways. Freud made one way famous: the so-called "slip" in which we betray ourselves by consciously unintended word or speech. But displaced confession can take other forms too. For instance, we "blurt": So driven are we by the urge to get things off our chests that we share guilty details of our lives with anyone who will listen. In its diarist mode, this kind of confession is associated with writers like Anaïs Nin. In its broadcast mode, it is the staple of talk shows like *Jerry Springer*, which has featured guests with such edifying disclosures as "I Married a Horse." But the tell-all never tells all; such confessions are always more or less dishonest. We may admit every detail of what we have done, *except that it was wrong*. Or we may make certain moral concessions, but only to divert attention from "the weightier points of the law." We may tell even our cruelest or most wanton deeds, but treat something else about them as more important—perhaps their beauty, or perhaps how unhappy we are.

Blurting is often misunderstood as shamelessness. It would better be considered evidence of shame. People unburdened by bad conscience do not tell all; normal human beings are more modest about their personal affairs, especially before strangers. But the crucial point about confession is that when it is not in the service of repentance, it remains in the service of sin, and to see this more clearly we must consider another kind of displaced confession: confession as advocacy.

There is nothing surprising about the fact that personal testimony can be an engaging way to advance a moral cause. Everyone likes to hear a story, and a well-told tale has the further advantage that it makes dry and difficult ideas come alive. "I know so-and-so is wrong, because I did it. This is what happened to me. Don't follow the example of my fall; follow the example of my recovery." The astonishing thing is that confession can be used to advance an *immoral* cause. "I know they say so-

and-so is wrong, but it must be right, because I suffered so much from not doing it."

For two reasons, confessions can be even more persuasive in bad causes than in good ones. In the first place, being fallen creatures ourselves, we sympathize with sin more easily than with goodness. In the second place, distorted confessions may be told with greater zeal than honest ones. A person who has already repented and thrown himself on the mercy of God may no longer need to confess; the need to tell the story has been satisfied already. If he does tell the story, he now tells it less for himself than for others. But for the unrepentant man, the opposite is true. His heart is still hot, and the need to confess is still fiery. He tells his story to appease his conscience; because he is unrepentant, he tells it crookedly; because conscience is not in fact appeased, he must tell it again and again.

Such stories may be given either of two different endings: the happy ending, "Now I follow my heart, and the sun has come up again," or the pathetic ending, "I followed my heart, but they were cruel to me; lend me yours." Both endings exploit our pity, but in different ways. The former exploits our pity for the sad former state of the confessing party, because we do not want to make him sad again. The latter exploits our pity for his sad present state, because we wish that his sorrows might be soothed. A good example of the happy sort of confession is the homosexual "coming out" story, which has become something of a cultural fixture. The pathetic sort of confession is illustrated by *But What If She Wants to Die?* by George E. Delury. Delury's wife suffered from multiple sclerosis, but had some years yet to live. After giving her a lethal dose of pills and suffocating her with a plastic bag, he served time in prison and is now an advocate of assisted suicide and euthanasia.

No one should underestimate the gravitational attraction of confessional advocacy of evil. The tale of the Delury murder is a case in point. He admits, denies, and dismisses his remorse, all at once. Immediately after describing the killing, he writes:

This act was at the base of a primitive, irrational guilt that haunted me for months after Myrna's death. It was not a moral guilt, an awareness of having done something ethically wrong; it was more immediate than that, almost physical. . . . I have come to believe we humans, like other primates, have an instinctual block against killing our own kind, a prohibition that, if violated, sets up strong undercurrents of dissonance. . . . I suspect that after the victorious animal finishes celebrating his or her survival and victory or comprehends the fact of death in an accident, an observer might see some unusual behavior—withdrawal, heightened sensitivity to slights or threats, increased rejection or acceptance of grooming, nervousness, and a host of other possible signs of uneasiness. It was this sort of primordial, instinctual unease that I felt and called "guilt." In the weeks and months that followed, I often spoke of my guilt feelings, trying to sort out their natures and sources. Listeners misunderstood, thinking I was referring to the act of helping Myrna die. But I had no moral guilt about the act itself, only about how I had handled it, about the silence. And, at other times, I was referring to this primitive guilt, the dissonance of a primate over the violation of a fundamental instinct.[9]

Notice the pattern of the argument. The remorse was not too weak to signify, but too strong: too immediate, too primordial, almost physical. But conscience is a mere product of my opinions, so nothing so powerful could be conscience!

In similar fashion, Delury both reports and denies his spiteful resentment toward his wife. At one point she suggests that they write a book together. His response is to write her a poison-pen letter:

I feel I am not being treated well. I feel that everyone is perfectly ready to see me die for your sake, but no one is prepared to do anything for my sake. And I am dying. I have only a few years left, ten at most, probably, but only two or three if my work load continues as it is. I too have a book to write, two books, and essays also. I have work to do, people to see, places to go. But no one asks about my needs.

I have fallen prey to the tyranny of a victim. You are sucking the life out of me like a vampire and nobody cares. In fact, it would appear that I am about to be cast in the role of villain because I no longer believe in you. Well, one can glower and glower and be a hero.

Here is how he explains to his readers the venomous epistle: "The last sentence, of course, is a reversal of Hamlet's, 'That one can smile and smile and be a villain.' Here, too, was the infamous 'vampire' phrase, pounced on by the DA and the press when they sought evidence of my heartlessness. I never tried to explain that the 'vampire' image originated with Myrna, who had begun to use it occasionally sometime the previous year, after seeing something about Ann Rice, the vampire novelist we had never read. Myrna had said she was like a vampire, living off other people's lives; I was reminding her of that point of view."[10]

It is difficult not to feel soiled after reading such sordid prose. Yet the allure of false confession is so strong that a reviewer for the *New York Times* wrote "This is a memoir that professes to be about death but is actually about love. . . . his portrait of a marriage is close to inspirational. . . . somehow the villains seem small next to this man's unquestioning love for his wife. . . . It is this book's love story, the story of two people who had something truly rare, that makes it interesting."[11]

THE THIRD FURY: ATONEMENT

The Third Fury draws its power from the knowledge of a debt which must somehow be paid. If we deny the debt, the knowledge works in us anyway, and we pay pain after pain, price after price, in a cycle which has no end because we refuse to pay the one price demanded. It is something like trying to fend off a loan shark. We pay the interest forever because we cannot pay off the principal, and the interest mounts.

In biblical reflection, the theme of false atonement is very old. The Psalmist implores the Author of his conscience,

> Deliver me from bloodguiltiness, O God, thou God of my salvation, and my tongue will sing aloud of thy deliverance. . . .
>
> For thou hast no delight in sacrifice; were I to give a burnt offering, thou wouldst not be pleased.
>
> The sacrifice acceptable to God is a broken spirit; a broken and contrite heart, O God, thou wilt not despise.[12]

Micah reaches the same conclusion. He asks, "with what shall I come before the Lord and bow myself before God on high? Shall I come before him with burnt offerings, with calves a year old? Will the Lord be pleased with thousands of rams, with ten thousands of rivers of oil? Shall I give my first-born for my transgression, the fruit of my body for the sin of my soul?" But none of these things can pay the price: "He has showed you, O man, what is good; and what does the Lord require of you but to do justice, and to love kindness, and to walk humbly with your God?"[13]

A broken and contrite heart—and then holiness. These things would pay the price, if I could give them. But what if I cannot?[14] Or what if I refuse? Then I am back to the treadmill—the futility of the calves, the rams, and the rivers of oil, of the fruit of my body for the sin of my soul.

With the rise of philanthropy, the rams, the calves, and the oil are no longer offered in the same way. The fruit of our bodies still is. In another book I told the story of a woman who aborted her first child to punish her unfaithful husband. Later she aborted her second one to punish herself. The one thing which could make her self-loathing greater yet was to increase her guilt; the one thing which could increase her guilt was to repeat the sin. As she explained to her counselor, "I wanted to be able to hate myself more for what I did to the first baby."

One suspects that such sacrifices are quite common. The goddess religions which feminists savor even ritualize them. Liturgies have been written for the sacrifice of children. Ginette Paris writes, "Our culture needs new rituals as well as laws to restore abortion to its sacred dimension, which is both terrible and necessary." She considers abortion "a sacrifice to Artemis," "a sacrament for the gift of life to remain pure."[15] Of course these are not presented as liturgies of false atonement, but no doubt they are.

Efforts to atone without repentance take other forms too. It was once expected that release of RU486 would generate a vast increase in the number of abortions because it is so much easier to swallow a pill than to undergo a surgical procedure. The facts are much different. As the study mentioned previously explains, RU486 can cause severe bleeding, cramping, and nausea, the expulsion of the embryo may take several days, and the woman may be able to recognize the remains of her child in the toilet or collection bucket. The dread of it all is that for some women these burdens are just what makes RU486 attractive. They welcome the suffering; they regard it as a price they ought to pay. The researchers describe one such case as follows: "Pauli's experience with mifepristone/ misoprestol dragged on for weeks; she bled heavily on and off, and eventually had to have an aspiration. She saw her prolonged experience as a sort of penance she was paying for the act of abortion. The 'miscarriage' did *not* go smoothly, so she couldn't maintain the fiction that what *was* happening to her was a miscarriage. . . . 'I just felt like this was happening because of what I'd done,' she said."[16]

A physician—the medical director at one of the locations conducting the trial—made the same observation. "There were a couple of cases of women who had a feeling that in a way they were sort of accepting their punishment for being pregnant because they would bleed more, they would have more pain." An LPN amended "a couple" to "a lot": "For some women I think it helped because it was a longer process. They were able to work through the guilt that they were feeling for terminating the pregnancy. A lot of that *mea culpa* stuff was, like, 'I am guilty. I am suffering. I am having more cramps. I am having more bleeding. I'm having more time to suffer over my choice in choosing this miscarriage rather than having an abortion.' A lot of women seemed to get real involved emotionally with that. And some it helped and some it didn't."[17]

"And some it helped and some it didn't"—is that true? False atonement may indeed "help" with the feelings of remorse; the problem is that it cannot actually atone, and so the need to atone comes screaming back—with the remorse or without it. One cannot repent something in the very act of doing it; suffering is not a *fee* which makes the deed all right. How many of these women then go on to find further punishments for themselves? To what further deeds are they driven? What are the consequences for their marriages, their families, their surviving children? Joan Appleton, a former NOW activist and head nurse at a Virginia abortion facility, reports that she used to ask herself why abortion "was such a psychological trauma for a woman, and such a difficult decision for a woman to make, if it was a natural thing to do. If it was so right, why was it so difficult?" She thought, "I counseled these women so well; they were so sure of their decision. Why are they coming back after me now—months and years later—psychological wrecks?"[18]

Needless to say, the phenomenon of false atonement is not restricted to abortion. Some instances are obvious, some not so obvious. One place to look is criminality. Dostoyevsky wrote that "legal punishment inflicted for a crime intimidates a criminal infinitely less than the lawmakers think, partly because *he himself morally demands it*."[19] A part of him wants to escape the penalty, but another part wants to be caught; he may commit his crimes carelessly just so he will be caught, or commit new ones because he has not yet been punished for the old. Another place to look is the secretive self-mutilation clinicians call "delicate self-cutting," which is increasingly common—like binging and purging—among adolescent girls. The usual sorts of theories are circulated. Maybe there is something wrong with their brain chemistry so that their frustration turns inward rather than out; maybe the pain relieves stress by causing their bodies to release endorphins; maybe the cutting increases their sense of control because they do it to themselves; and so on. Perhaps each theory is partly true. Certainly each is partly false. For why should self-cutting be on the *rise*? And why should it be especially common among girls who are sexually active? The one kind of guess which clinicians do not venture is the moral kind. There is no reason to think adolescent brain chemistry more disordered today than it ever was; but there is plenty more reason for adolescents today to be ashamed.

THE FOURTH FURY: RECONCILIATION

Human beings are not like the fabled Cyclopes, who lived to themselves. We are designed for a partnership in good life with our kind. Because transgression casts us out of the partnership, one of the first effects of guilty knowledge is loneliness and a need to reconcile. If we refuse to restore the bonds we have broken, then we must find substitutes. Thieves seek thieves for company; drunks seek drunks; molesters seek molesters. Just because these bonds are counterfeit, they cannot satisfy the need for reconciliation, so it presses us harder still.

The graver the transgression, the wider the gulf between the transgressor and humane society—and the deeper the sense of significance with which the substitute bonds must be imbued. People who have participated in euthanasia or assisted suicide often say that they have never before been so close to another human being; the severing of bonds gives them a stronger sense of intimacy than the forming of them. "This is the true union," the burdened mind insists; "this is not death, but true life." It might seem impossible that a counterfeit intimacy based on shared guilt could be more attractive than the real thing, but some people find it so. In his study of Dutch euthanasia, psychologist Herbert Hendin finds that doctors and nurses are drawn into the movement just to achieve it.[20] The same allure, the same false intimacy, draws people into gangs and death squads, except that in this case the counterfeit bond is formed not with victims but with fellow perpetrators. The groups themselves understand quite well that their unity is grounded on shared guilt; making sure that it is shared is the bedrock of their policy. Robert J. Lifton reports that among the Nazi death camp doctors, the bond with the group was sealed with "blood cement" (*Blutkitt*), meaning "direct participation in the group's practice of killing"—a policy, he observes, which criminal groups have long followed throughout the world. Nothing bonds the group like mortal sin. Or so it seems.

The need for reconciliation also explains why the movements for disordered sexuality—homosexual, pederastic, sadomasochistic—cannot be satisfied with toleration, but must propagandize, recruit, and convert. They do not suffer from sexual deprivation, for partners are easy enough to find. They suffer from social deprivation, because they are cut off from the everyday bonds of life. They want to belong; they want to belong as they are; there can be only one solution. Society must reconcile with *them*. The shape of human life must be transformed. All of the assumptions of normal sexuality must be dissolved: marriage, family, innocence, purity, childhood—all must be called into question, even if it means pulling down the world around their ears. The same thing happened in another great controversy a century and a half ago. "Why did the slaveholders act as if driven by the Furies to their own destruction?" asks John Thomas Noonan: "Why did they take such risks, why did they persist beyond prudent calculation? The answer must be that in a moral question of this kind, turning on basic concepts of humanity, you cannot be content that your critics are feeble and ineffective, you cannot be content with their practical tolerance of your activities. You want, in a sense you need, actual acceptance, open approval. If you cannot convert your critics by argument, at least by law you can make them recognize that your course is the course of the country."[21]

But guilty solidarity has a quiet and domestic side too. "How could Mary get mixed up with a man like that?" One answer is that his being "like that" may have been the pivot of his attraction. The issue here is not the allure of the forbidden *as such,* but the charm of the prospect of sharing it. Let us suppose that John has a disreputable secret. He unburdens himself to Mary—"I could never tell this to anyone but you"— and asks for her complicity and understanding. Or he makes an indecent proposal to her; the effect may be very much the same. Naturally, she is repelled. On the other hand, sharing the secret may give her a sense of intimacy, and the fact that it is a guilty one makes it only more intimate still. She has been invited to enter a chamber—nay, she is there—where the rest of the world, she thinks, can never come. Curiously, then, the guiltiness of what John has to say is precisely what he employs to attract her. Guilt is his "line." It may not succeed with most women, but it succeeds often enough to keep him trying.

THE FIFTH FURY: JUSTIFICATION

In English, "to justify" can mean to *make* something just, to *show* that it is just, to *maintain* that it is just, or to *feign* that it is just. The striking thing is that the first and fourth meanings are exactly opposed. According to the first, I am justified when I am finally brought in line with justice. According to the fourth, I am justified when "justice" is finally brought in line with me. Guilty knowledge demands the former; we attempt to appease it, however, by means of the latter. We rationalize. We make excuses. We preserve the form of the law without its substance.

Of all the games we play with the Five Furies, our game with the Fifth is perhaps most dangerous. No one has ever discovered a way to merely set aside the moral law; what the rationalizer must do is make it appear that he is *right*. Rationalizations, then, are powered by the same moral law which they twist. With such mighty motors, defenses of evil pull away from us; we are compelled to defend not only the original guilty deed, but others which it was no part of our intention to excuse. At one point in the Congressional debate over partial-birth abortion, when a senator who opposed a ban was asked at what point in the birth process a baby acquires a right not to be killed, she replied "when you bring your baby home." It was only one of several inconsistent positions that she took during questioning, but no matter; it shows how the justifications that we employ for our deeds take on a life of their own. Others have been more consistent. Medical infanticide has already quietly begun. Who buys the premises must pay the conclusions.[22]

Consider the way the sexual revolution metastasized. It all began when we decided to dispense with chastity. Now that was not easy to do; there had always been unchaste *behavior*, recognized as wrong, but this was different. For the protection of the procreative partnership, sex had hitherto been a culturally recognized privilege of marriage. Dispensing with chastity required destroying this privilege. But one thing leads to another; to destroy the marital privilege requires denying what sex is *for*. It has to be separated first from procreation and second from the particular intimacy that arises from the procreative partnership and is inseparable from it.

Now no one can really be oblivious to the deep claims of these goods. To set them aside, powerful magic is necessary. One must invoke another strong good against them; the moral structure must be distorted so that it can be set against itself. And so the genie of happiness was summoned to the task. But this was not easy to do either; as Samuel Johnson said, "Almost all the miseries of life, almost all the wickedness that infects society, and almost all the distresses that afflict mankind, are the consequences of some defect in private duties. Likewise, all the joys of this world may be attributable to the happiness of hearth and home."[23] It could not be *that* happiness which was invoked, or the goods of marriage would not be defeated. Comprehensive happiness had to be confused with sexual pleasure. Sexual pleasure, moreover, had to be asserted not just as a good but as a *right,* so that all the moral force of justice could be conjured on its behalf. My right implies your duty.

By itself, a right to sex might mean only a right to perform the act—with a responsibility to bear the consequences. A right to sexual pleasure, on the other hand, is a much grander thing, because it confers *exemption* from certain consequences. I therefore have a right to contraception, because a baby might be a burden. Should contraception fail, I have a right to an abortion. Should my girlfriend not want to abort, well, that's her lookout. She has a right not to get one, but I have a right not to hear the word "Daddy."

Amazingly, women accepted this line. Or maybe not so amazingly, for like the men, they had accepted the reasoning that led up to it; to reject it would be to admit that they had been wrong. Even so, the "fun" stage of the sexual revolution was now over. Men and women came to seem less like the old jam and bread than like predator and prey, and the old mockery "All's fair in love and war" became redundant; love became a great deal like war. And if men *had* become enemies, then women *had* to get abortions—didn't they?

Another problem was that with procreation out and abortion in, the meaning of sexuality had flipped over from giving life to taking it. It is much harder to justify killing than sleeping around. We can't not know that it is wrong to deliberately take innocent human life; parsing the rule, we find only six possibilities of rationalization. All of them have been tried, but what do they do to us? Where will they take us next?

     1   It is wrong to *deliberately* take innocent human life. But I didn't mean for this to happen; I wasn't trying to get pregnant.

The reasoning here is that if something happens that I don't want, then no matter what I do about it, I am not responsible. This destroys the very idea of personal responsibility, and therewith any possibility of leading a coherent life. It is a formula for personal chaos.

2   It is wrong to deliberately *take* innocent human life. But I'm not taking life, the doctors are doing it. This is just something happening to me. I'm not involved.

This time the reasoning is that once I have made a decision, the results are out of my hands—even if they were planned and intended. To think this way one must almost say "I am not me." Longfellow wrote "as in a building stone rests on stone, and wanting the foundation all would be wanting, so in human life each action rests on the foregoing event that made it possible, but is forgotten and buried in the earth."[24] But an evil deed cannot be buried in the earth; it can only be buried in the mind, unquiet, undead.

3   It is wrong to deliberately take *innocent* human life. But the fetus isn't innocent; it makes a woman pregnant.

Hatred of human nature is the premise of the third rationalization—especially of female nature. The sole purpose of the uterus is to home and house the baby, who has no place else to go. Yet the baby is here regarded as a trespasser, almost as a rapist.[25] Although it is hard to imagine an actual woman taking this view, some abortion proponents consider it quite promising, perhaps because judges will believe things that most women will not. As one feminist writes, "the fetus is not innocent but instead aggressively intrudes on a woman's body so massively that deadly force is justified to stop it." She admits that "Few people are going to be comfortable with the idea," but says this shows how not only the law, but also culture and public opinion must change.[26]

4   It is wrong to deliberately take innocent *human* life. But it's not

human—it can't feel, it can't think, it can't communicate—and how could it be human if it's so small?

Among pro-abortion philosophers, this rationalization is by far the most popular.[27] The reasoning is that human personhood, *who-ness,* depends on criteria like sensitivity, intelligence, and self-awareness, and the fetus is just a *what.* Of course born people too can be more or less sensitive, more or less intelligent, more or less self-aware. By this reasoning, born people too must be unequally endowed with personhood— some more, some less. The only question is whom we shall have as our masters. At the top may be those with the most exquisite feelings, the most complex thoughts, the keenest sense of self—it all depends. I think I know who these scholars have in mind.

> 5   It is wrong to deliberately take innocent human *life.* But it's not
>   alive, not truly. It's more like a blood clot. Or like my period
>   just won't come down.

Such a thing would have been easier to believe before the discovery of the nature of conception. It takes a ferocious act of denial to go on believing it in the age of ultrasound. Blood clots do not roll over and suck their thumbs.

> 6   It is *wrong* to deliberately take innocent human life. But some-
>   times you have to do what's wrong.

This is the most disturbing rationalization of all, because it embraces the wrong with eyes open. The temptation is ancient: "Let us do evil that good may result." Some men and women involved in abortion promise themselves to repent later. Unfortunately, repentance cannot be planned, but only performed; to promise repentance later is to harden the heart *now,* and perhaps destroy the capacity to repent. Others who have participated in abortion promise themselves to "make up for it." To do this is merely to call down the Third Fury of false atonement. One can certainly pay a price. One may pay many prices. But it does not pay *the* price.

No wonder that in the present stage of the revolution that began with sex we go on past abortion and explore other kinds of killing, like infanticide and the slaying of the weak, the old, and the sick. You cannot justify one evil yet expect the others to keep their place. The cloth of the moral law is too tightly sewn for that; it is made of a single strand. Pluck loose one stitch, and the rest unravels too. "We're not hurting anyone," we used to say; but then we hurt. Short of penitence, we can never stop. Driven to justify one sin, we are driven to justify the next. If we have already reached killing, what comes next?

THE PURPOSE OF THE FURIES

Avenging conscience explains the remark of G. K. Chesterton: "Men may keep a sort of level of good, but no man has ever been able to keep on one level of evil. That road goes down and down."[28] Pursued by the Five Furies, a man becomes both more wicked and more stupid: more wicked because his behavior becomes worse, more stupid because he tells himself more lies.

This downward spiral may seem to reveal a flaw in the design of conscience. Shouldn't it drive us up, not down? Not necessarily. As Dante found, for some of us the road up goes down for a long time first. The system of conscience has not broken; it has merely merged into the system of natural consequences. This is fully compatible with its mission. After all, the greater purpose of conscience is not to inform us of moral truth, but to motivate us to live by it. For most of us at some times, for some of us at most times, guilty knowledge is not exhortation enough. Drastic measures become necessary. Driving life out of kilter is, so to speak, the exhortation of last resort. The offender becomes stupider and wickeder—but then he had intended to become stupider and wickeder; that is what obstinacy and denial are all about. His only hope is to become even stupider and wickeder than he had planned. If all goes well he may finally be so wretched that he comes "to himself"—or to God. Apparently, for the chance to soften a heart, the Designer is even willing that it become more rocklike still. In this life, what has been called "the left hand of God" may be, in reality, the left hand of His mercy.

This is a staggering reflection for those who think of God as a tooth fairy. Less drastic means of turning a soul around can certainly be imagined. Probably, though, no less drastic means of turning a soul around are compatible with free will, which seems to be one of His design criteria. We may find the price too high, because in order to escape the Furies a man may inflict terrible damage on other people. What this suggests is that the Designer thinks scarcely any price too high to save a soul. Even souls may be risked to save a soul. Yet other souls may be risked to save those.[29]

8

Eclipse

*How other factors have contributed
to the eclipse of the natural law.*

I N A SOLAR ECLIPSE, the moon intervenes so that the sun can no longer be seen. Even so its influence continues: we remain in the sun's field of gravity, and an angry corona can be seen around the black edges of the obscuring lunar disk. So too with the eclipse of the natural law. When our wills intervene so that our hearts are put in shadow, we do not cut off all of its influence; we only render that influence dreadful to ourselves.

So far I have discussed the eclipse of the natural law mainly from the perspective of individual conscience. But how does it come about that an entire culture passes into the shadow? Such things are not well understood, yet a few obvious things can be said about our own case.

THE ATROPHY OF TRADITION

Earlier I explained that the fact that there is a natural law does not make moral education redundant; moral education reinforces, elicits, guards, builds upon, and confronts us about what we know already. I have also explained that one of the most important ways this takes place is through sound tradition. To some people in our day the word "tradition" suggests merely a repeated action which is hallowed by sentimental associations, like wearing a certain tartan or eating turkey on a certain day. I mean a good deal more than that—a shared way of life which molds the mind, character, and imagination of those who practice it, for better or for worse. It is a sort of apprenticeship in living, with all of the previous generations as masters, and includes not only ways of doing things, but ways of raising questions about things that matter. Not that the tartans and the turkey are irrelevant. The point of the tartan is to identify me as a member of my clan and distinguish me from the members of all others, thereby reinforcing a way of life in which my primary duties are to people whom I have not chosen but who are unalterably chosen for me by birth. The point of the turkey is to celebrate and share the bounty of God, thereby teaching me gratitude, piety, generosity, and confident faith.

In our time many people are traditionless. Of course this is but a way of speaking, for scorn of traditions can itself be transmitted traditionally, and it is. Traditionlessness, then, is not the absence of traditions so much as a particular, unsound sort of tradition which does not recognize itself as tradition, disbelieves whatever it does recognize as tradition, and is traditionally smug about its disbelief. It is the absence, not of traditions as such, but of sound ones. In other times and places, traditions have gone bad in other ways. In ours, it happens this way.

Consider for example traditionlessness in religion. A good many parents decline to give their children any religious instruction, saying that they think it is better to "let them make up their own minds." But declining to teach is itself a way of teaching, a very effective one, and it teaches children a very definite creed with eight articles: (1) It is not important for children to know anything about God. (2) The questions which children naturally ask about Him require no answers. (3) Parents know nothing about Him worth passing on. (4) To think about Him adequately, no preparation is needed. (5) What adults think about Him makes no difference. (6) By implication, He does not make any difference either; God is not to be treated as God. (7) If anything is to be treated as God, it will have to be something other than Him. (8) This is the true creed, and all other creeds are false.

In general, a person who has been raised in a sound tradition is far better prepared to change his mind, should his beliefs prove faulty in some particular respect, than a person who has been raised "to make up his own mind" about them. While the former has at least acquired some equipment—the habit of taking important things seriously, and a body of inherited reflections about what some of these things are—the latter is weighed down with different baggage: the habit of *not* taking important things seriously, and the habit of considering the way things really are as less important than what he thinks of them at the moment.

But there are other things that make sound tradition difficult in our time besides the tradition of making it difficult. The vigor of sound traditions requires a way of life in which the generations live in close proximity and have discourse with each other. It requires that people in general live in communities in which they know each other and can hold each other accountable. It requires that in relations among the various cultural institutions—parents, churches, schools, government and so forth—the agents higher on the totem pole regard themselves merely as servants of the lower, and not as their masters or competitors. Unfortunately, the lines along which our own society is organized are diametrically opposed to these. The generations say little to each other, and may be hundreds of miles apart. Nearly one out of five people changes his residence each year. Under such circumstances it is hardly surprising that the cultural institutions higher on the totem pole assume that they "know better" and try to gobble up the functions of the lower. The fact that shreds of sound tradition do survive is cause for wonder.

THE CULT OF THE EXPERT

I have remarked more than once that the natural law expresses the common sense of plain people everywhere. If this is true, then one would expect it to shine out with particular brightness today, for the modern age is supposed to be the age of the common man. This is a myth. The modern age is not the age of the common man; it is the age of the expert. The rule of experts is understandable in specialized fields like computers and open heart surgery, but we make it the rule in every department of life. No one understands law but the lawyer, no one understands policy but the bureaucrat, no one understands ethics but the ethicist. There are no wise men any more, but only therapists. When all of life is dissolved into specialized fields, something is wrong. Why has this happened? How has it come about that the common man has lost his place in the "age of the common man"? Perhaps the chief reason is philosophical.[1]

Modern thought is much more elitist than ancient thought, though it talks a less elitist line. In both eras the great philosophers recognized that some men have greater understanding than others. The difference is that in ancient thought the ideal is the man of wisdom, whereas in modern thought the ideal is the man of expertise. Aristotle belonged to the old school. Though he pursued wisdom, he began all of his ethical reflections by considering what ordinary people think all over the world. Even on those occasions when he considered the opinions of sages, they were the men whom ordinary people themselves recognized as sages. Of course, to begin with common sense is not the same as to end there. Indeed, in particular times and places the common sense of plain people can be corrupted, and I comment on such corruptions later in the chapter, because they make the path of the natural law much rockier. Even so, the wisdom of the philosopher lay mainly in his grasp of the deep presuppositions and remote implications of our universal common sense, not in something completely alien to it; what he tried to understand is what the common sense is *getting at*. The ideal was that when the philosopher had finished his work, the common man would say "Yes, that is what I wanted to say, but I didn't know how." This is also the deepest goal of medieval reflections on the natural law, and it is even biblical. There is, to be sure, a direct divine revelation which we cannot do without. And yet as St. Paul said, a law is written even on the hearts of the gentiles, however it may be suppressed.

By contrast, in the modern period the thread connecting the highest thoughts of the philosopher with the plain sense of the common man is stretched so thin that it finally breaks. The ancients thought common folk knew something—but in a general and confused sort of way. In an incredible passion of hubris, Descartes thought that in the strict sense the common folk have *no knowledge whatsoever*, and that before himself, all philosophers have been in the same boat. The reason for this, he says, is that true knowledge is something *certain*, and no one before him has had a right to be certain about anything; what they have had is not knowledge, but merely opinion. To attain certainty, he proposes that all opinion be passed through a sort of certification engine of his own devising. The engine he devised was systematic doubt. Whatever can be doubted, should be doubted; no starting point should be accepted unless it literally cannot be doubted. This was the point of his celebrated line, "I think, therefore I am." In his own existence, he believed that he had finally found something that could survive his own intellectual meat grinder, for he could not doubt his own existence; if he was thinking, he existed! Alas, this didn't work. I can doubt that there is thought; I can doubt that thinking requires a thinker; I can doubt anything whatsoever. So if certainty requires something that literally cannot be doubted, then the certification engine devised by Descartes has failed. But even though his engine failed, his precedent stood. What the modern era decided that it had learned from Descartes is simply this: nothing counts as real knowledge until experts—be they lawyers, bioethicists, educational psychologists, or what have you—have passed it through a certification engine. Which certification engine the experts use (and there are many) is no longer considered particularly important. What counts is that there is a certification engine, which none but the experts understand.

THE RETURN OF THE SOPHIST

Although natural law must be applied to changing circumstances, it reflects unchanging truth. Nothing we can do can make it right to kill my neighbor; no twist of circumstance can make it unnecessary to keep faith with my wife. God is to be honored though the heavens fall, the seas dry up, and the mountains crumble to dust. In the fifth century BC, however, a group of thinkers appeared in Greece who maintained that just because circumstances change, there is no unchanging truth. These were the Sophists, paid teachers of rhetoric, whose boast was that they could teach anyone to argue any side of any question.

It was a "useful" skill. In Athens and the other democratic cities, democracy did not mean what it does to us. Modern constitutional democracy of the American sort is really more like what Aristotle called "polity," mixed government, but ennobled by the recognition that human beings bear the image of God; it means that many groups share power on principles of equal dignity, institutional balance, and natural justice. Though we speak of majority rule, the majority is supposed to rule by reason, not by whim, and there are things which even the majority is forbidden from doing. Though a large and impassioned majority can break through any check, this takes time, and the hope of the Framers was that in time even the hottest majority would cool. By contrast, ancient democracy meant that the most numerous group or class could do as it pleased. Thousands might attend the Assembly of the People. Hundreds might constitute a jury. Whoever had the knack of swaying the mob became a demagogue, and this was the knack which the Sophists claimed to teach.

The underlayer of the Sophists' training was a certain view of reality—a paradoxical view, because ultimately it denied reality. Man is the measure of all things, but man has no fixed nature. Man measures all things by his words, but words have no fixed meanings. Language is not an instrument for finding truth, but for changing it. Those who can master it, master all. It is a good creed for rogues, and commends itself to tyrants in every age.

Like ours. Among our own experts, Sophism is all the rage, except that it is no longer called Sophism. These days it prefers longer names, like "postmodernism," "epistemological relativism", and "antifoundationalism". They come to much the same thing. *Postmodernism* is "suspicion of metanarratives." Everyone tells himself a story about how the world seems to him; a metanarrative is a Big Story that tries to make sense of how it really is. Suspicion of metanarratives, then, means thinking that no one ever gets the Big Story right. But then postmodernists too have a Big Story: that no one ever gets it right. In which case, since no one ever gets it right, their story must be wrong. *Epistemological relativism* is the view that truth is relative to one's point of view. In other words, there is no Truth with a capital T, but only your truth (true only from your point of view), and my truth (true only from mine). In architecture, this would correspond to the proposition that because the house looks different from the east and from the west, there is no house. If we ask an epistemological relativist from which point of view epistemological relativism is true, only one answer is possible: from his own. But it is not true from any other point of view, so we may dismiss it. *Antifoundationalism* is the view that there are no first principles. Everything goes around in circles. We believe in A because of B, B because of c, c because of A—and that's okay. Just don't ask the antifoundationalist how he knows it's okay, because he assumes this as a first principle.

Sophism has always been a corrupter of democracies, and the difference between ancient and modern Sophism corresponds to the difference between ancient and modern democracy. Ancient democracy was radical democracy, so in order to win power through the sophistical arts, one had to win over the Assemblies of the People. Modern democracy is constitutional democracy, full of checks and balances, so there are other possibilities. The Sophists might seize power, not in the assemblies, but in the courts and the civil service; in this case the assemblies might not have to be wholly corrupted, but only confused enough to go along.

In our own polity this strategy is well advanced, especially in the courts. When the U.S. Supreme Court declared that "At the heart of liberty is the right to define one's own concept of existence, of meaning, of the universe, and of the mystery of human life,"[2] it was expressing the Sophist charter. In the context in which it was uttered, the purpose of the statement was to justify the liberty to kill unborn babies. Taken at its face, however, such language can justify doing anything you please. It's true that I flew a jet airliner into the World Trade Center, but I was defining my concept of existence. It's true that I raped my neighbor, but I was working out my concept of meaning in the universe as I see it. It's true that I drowned my toddlers, but I was fulfilling my concept of the mystery of human life. If the Supreme Court has not yet drawn these conclusions, it hardly matters. The conclusions follow from the Court's premises.

If Sophists are to run the courts and the civil service, they need plenty of help. From somewhere there must come a steady stream of people who think as they do, to fill vacancies as they open up. Universities fill this need. Ordinary people who have not spent time on college campuses find it difficult to believe just how thoroughly they subvert the mind and how little they train it. When the average person tunes in to a news and interview program and hears Professor Prevalent compare terrorists with policemen, dismiss the teaching of Western Civilization, or explain why a crackdown on live sex performances would have a chilling effect on free speech, he tends to have thoughts like the following: "He couldn't have said what I thought he said," "There must be something here that I don't understand," "He couldn't be typical of university professors," "Thank God my kid's teachers aren't like that," or "My kid wouldn't be taken in anyway." The correct responses are that he probably did, there probably isn't, he certainly is, they probably are, and he probably is already.

The curriculum of the university is but a tithe of what it teaches. It is a total-immersion counterculture whose methods of indoctrination include classroom style, freshman orientation, speech codes, mandatory diversity training, dormitory policies, guidelines for registered student organizations, mental health counseling, and peer pressure. Not all faculty and administrators are quite like Professor Prevalent. Some are even more extreme, and some, of course, are less. But if the modern university is not theoretically Sophist, it is operationally Sophist, and the extremists hold the high ground. Faculty who think differently are ashamed to oppose them, and administrators who do are afraid to rock the boat.

THE INFANTILE REGRESSION OF PUBLIC REFLECTION

The third generation of television babies is now coming of age. Mine was lucky. In our childhood television still imitated books; now books imitate television. Worse: Television programs imitate television advertisements. Once upon a time even an advertisement had to tell a story. But the true power of the medium has been discovered, and now they present only montages of half-second images, too short for reflective intelligence. Product descriptions have shrunk to grunts like "Uh-huh."

The way that we talk about important things is very much the same. Few people read. More books are sold than ever, but the ones that sell are mostly coffee table books or companions to exercise videos. Attention spans shrink from want of exercise. Political candidates avoid issues rather than engaging them; their strategy is not to persuade, but to "activate the base"—to arouse the voting groups which are presumed to be persuaded already. When I ask my graduating college students to "formulate an argument," I have to tell them what I mean. Many of them have never heard the expression; the idea of persuading someone by reasoning is new to them. They conceive an opinion as a kind of taste, like a partiality for one brand of soft drink over another. Many of my colleagues will tell them that they are right. The notion of the common good is yet more remote; a young woman in one of my classes needed it explained to her again and again. She told me she had always been taught that politics expresses self-interest; never before had anyone suggested that her views of public affairs, or those of anyone else, might ever reflect something else.

Now it is not necessary to read in order to thoughtfully participate in traditions of reflection about how we ought to live. The people of pre-literate societies had capacious memories for complex oral tradi- tions that held the place that books once held for us. Torah, for example, was passed down by word of mouth for generations before being set down in writing. Post-literate societies like ours are the ones that present the problem. One must do either a lot of reading or a lot of listening to participate in traditions of reflection, and in either case, a lot of remem- bering. The people of our time do none of these things. Instead we look at sparkling pictures that appear for a moment, then vanish.

A picture is worth a thousand words, we say. That is a highly equivo- cal proverb. If a picture merely illustrates a story, then the story can be as long and complex as we like. But if the whole burden of the tale is on the picture, then the tale had better be a simple one, or no one will understand it. Still less can a picture develop an argument. To set forth a syllogism, to draw out a distinction, to clear up a confusion, we need words. Nothing else will do.

To be sure, there are ways to increase an image's power. Through its symbolism, the frontispiece of Thomas Hobbes' *Leviathan* is arguably worth many thousand words. Looming over a well-ordered city and countryside is a crowned sovereign, gargantuan in his dimensions. He wears a mail shirt, but the links of his mail are the subjects of the commonwealth, of whom he is composed. In one hand he holds a sword, in the other a bishop's crozier, showing that he unites the civil and ecclesiastical power. To drive the point home, the title of the book is flanked by pairs of smaller images, left and right, civil and ecclesiastical, beneath the sword and the crozier respectively: castle and church, coronet and mitre, cannon of war and thunderbolt of excommunication, matching armories of physical and dialectical weapons, military battle and theological disputation. Topping the whole is the Latin motto *Non Est potestas Super Terram quae Comparetur ei*—"There is no power on earth which can be compared with him"—a passage from Job 41 in the Vulgate. Yet although these symbols vastly enlarge the power of the picture to remind us of Hobbes' argument, they cannot enable it to take its place. We still need the book; without it virtually all of the meaning is lost. Who is the enormous figure? Is he threatening the land or protecting it? And why are little people crawling on him? They might be maggots.

Our pictures are not like that anyway. Having become verbally illiterate, we have also become visually illiterate. The images which make up our daily fare are designed neither to remind us of the steps of an argument, like *Leviathan*'s frontispiece, nor to illustrate the stages of a story, like a row of stained glass windows, but to elicit unseemly desires: avarice, envy, lust, and all the rest. These sell.

I would say it were as though a great fire had consumed all our books and memories, except that it is more like a great smoke which fills our houses and dulls our minds and makes it difficult to complete any thoughts. There is hope. The young woman who had never heard of a good above selfishness could hardly stop asking about it. When Nehemiah read the Law to the returning exiles, they wept with longing. We are put together in such a way that although we can be pushed and pulled and drowsied by flickering images, we cannot be satisfied by them; we know too much even in oblivion. Fallow knowledge troubles our sleep. We lie under the prickling enchantment of the image carved into our hearts, which is stronger than the counterspell and can never be quite scratched out.

THE DISABLING OF SHOCK AND SHAME

Everything bad puts something normal to abnormal use. Consider for example the natural process of desensitization. When a particular stimulus is presented to a creature many times, gradually its response becomes weaker. This phenomenon can be observed across a wide range of organisms, even those without central nervous systems. Touch a hydra without hurting it, and it flinches. Touch it again, and it flinches again. Touch it fifty times, and by the fiftieth touch the flinch is much less pronounced. Eventually the hydra stops flinching. Desensitization is one of the variety of ways by which an organism fine-tunes its responses to make them more appropriate to its environment; it "learns" which stimuli are more important and which are less, becoming more sensitive to the former and less to the latter. Without the capacity for desensitization, an organism subjected to continuous unimportant stimuli would become exhausted.

All such provisions in the design of our physical faculties have counterparts in the design of our deliberative faculties. Someone threatens me. As the shock of adrenalin races through my body, another shock of readiness races through my mind. Quickly I make plans to meet his violence. But nothing happens. He threatens me again. Again nothing happens. By the fiftieth threat, I have realized that he is all talk and no action, and I all but ignore him.

But the adaptive system can be fooled. The latest fad in the world of toys is action figures of pop musicians. With the Alice Cooper figure produced by McFarlane Toys comes a miniature guillotine, the singer's severed head, and a little basket to catch it in. The Eminem figure from Art Asylum is screaming and swinging a chainsaw, his face distorted with rage and malice. But the best is yet to come: the next Eminem release will include a dead woman in a car trunk, memorializing the lyrics and cover of his first album. It will be said that these toys are not intended for children, but that is not what the manufacturers say. Art Asylum's promotional literature declares that "The traditional jack-in-the-box, once the king of every kid's toy box, is being reinvented for the 21st Century."[3] Its slogan is "Psycho Toyz for Crazy Kidz," and they are, in fact, sold in some toy stores. Then again, why not? As one music critic explains to us, the rapper is merely "one of those charming rogues"—"indubitably dangerous" but "exceptionally witty," "thoughtful," and "good-hearted." This by way of comment on another Eminem album, the lyrics of which concern incest with his mother.[4]

How is it possible to tolerate such things? According to the critic, you have to "disable your prejudgment button." Prejudgment means judging before the facts are in, but he isn't asking us to delay judgment about whether the music is evil; the evil he more or less concedes. Rather he is asking us to delay judgment about whether such evil can be fun. It has "immense entertainment value"—for a while. Needless to say, the same discovery has been made in the other media. A magazine sold in every convenience store has depicted a nude woman being fed into a meatgrinder and emerging as hamburger. "Mainstream" movies outdo the ancient Roman amphitheatre by showing every spurt of blood close up and ten feet tall. Video games allow the player to feel that every time a victim is stabbed, shot, dismembered, eviscerated, decapitated, or burned, he is doing the killing himself. Lust and gore beyond the dreams of cruelty fall into our cupped hands. Hardly a word of protest is heard; instead, "We need more research."

You see what has happened. We were touched by abomination, and we flinched. But nothing happened. We were touched again. Again nothing happened. By the five-hundredth touch, we stopped flinching.

But something did happen. We became the sort of people who endure the abominable touch. We may consider ourselves unchanged just because we do not all find torture games entertaining, but already we accept them as entertainment. We support a popular culture which mixes chainsaw massacres with music; we have raised a generation who consider it cool to think about dead women stuffed into car trunks. Inevitably some act out these fantasies—the thrill of merely imagining them palls—but that is not the point; even if none ever did, it would be bad enough. The damage has been done.

THE PROLONGATION OF ADOLESCENCE

If we think of adolescence as the span of time between the biological readiness to begin a family and the moral readiness to assume its responsibilities, it might seem that it should be very short—a brief walk through a corridor between one room of life to another. Until recently it was; adolescence as we know it is historically new.

Think of a time when the interval between puberty and marriage was much shorter than it is today. Most people worked the land, but great age is not needed to farm; other young men of common birth apprenticed at trades or went into commerce. Those of higher birth sometimes acquired various kinds of learning, but usually not at universities. Those who did matriculate at universities were few in number, often began when much younger than students today, and were frequently destined for holy orders—which meant, not marriage, but celibacy. Adolescence, as we know it, barely existed; people passed rather more quickly from childhood to adulthood, and did not expect an extended period of play in between. Various rituals dramatized the admission of the young person into the adult community. That society had problems of its own, but a long interval between the ability to marry and the entrance into matrimony was not one of them.

Something has happened. In the first place, all over the world the age of puberty is dropping. No one knows why, although guesses abound. One theory blames it on persistent organic pollutants—chemicals which mimic estrogen, released by industrial processes into the environment. Another blames it on what might be called cultural pollutants—the unavoidable and unremitting deluge of sexual stimulation in words, sounds, and images. Still others blame it on better nutrition, although it is hard to see why having sufficient food should be maladaptive.

In the second place, as the age of puberty drops, the age of marriage rises. Here some of the reasons are obscure, but not all of them. Many lines of work require more training than of old; that is plain enough. More puzzling is that apprenticeships have died out, and most training has been exported from the workplace to the school—where students earn no wages. Schools, in the meantime, have become incompetent, so that the time necessary to learn anything is much longer. What once was taught in secondary school now waits for college; what once was taught in college now waits for postgraduate school. The result is a long period of economic dependence.

Apologists for late marriage consider it good because human beings do not reach maturity until their mid-twenties. "To marry before this," says John R.W. Stott, "runs the risk of finding yourself at twenty-five married to somebody who was a very different person at the age of twenty."[5] Stott is a wise man from whom much can be learned, and I am loath to differ with him. Certainly people should not marry until they are mature. But the age at which people are mature enough to take on the responsibilities of marriage is not a human constant; it depends in part on *when we marry*. For centuries, most people married and began families in their teens. If today they are not ready until twenty-five— or thirty—or thirty-five—then our first question ought to be "Why aren't they?" We should also pause to remember how maturity is attained. Men and women do not first become mature, and then accept responsibilities; it is through accepting responsibilities that they become mature. Responsibility itself is what transforms them, the marital responsibility above most others. Matrimony shatters and reassembles two people into a single organism with two personalities. If you marry at twenty, then you *ought* to be very different persons at twenty-five—and you ought to have changed hand in hand. Unfortunately, the older we become, the harder it is to yield to the transformation; the more nearly we have finished our changes, the harder it is for us to change.

The unnatural prolongation of adolescence poses a variety of moral problems. Normal erotic desire is transmuted from a spur to marriage to an incentive for promiscuity. Promiscuity thwarts the attainment of moral wisdom, and makes conjugal love itself seem unattractive. Furthermore, prolonged irresponsibility is itself a sort of training, and a bad one. Before long the entire culture is caught up in a Peter Pan syndrome, terrified of leaving childhood. At this point even the responsibilities of marriage and family begin to lose their transformative character. Men in their forties with children in their twenties say "I still don't feel like a grown-up," "I still can't believe I'm a father." Their very capacity to face the moral life has been impaired.

THE CULT OF FEELINGS

The last great reason for the eclipse of the natural law is bondage to the emotions, which requires a somewhat lengthier explanation. "O for a Life of Sensations rather than of Thoughts!" wrote John Keats.[6] This wish has passed into pop culture. At the climax of the *Star Wars* movie, a spectral voice warns the hero, "Luke! Trust your feelings!" The cover of a hugely popular self-help book declares, "with no effort other than paying attention to how we're feeling, we can mold our lives exactly as we choose with relative ease and speed."[7] One would think that the world were in thrall to cold deliberation, and our only hope were to get back in touch with our feelings. This is like trying to revive a drunk with vodka. We are not out of touch with our feelings, but infatuated by them.

The adoration of feelings is quite ecumenical, and comes in seven varieties. First is ROMANTICISM, the cult of ecstatic feelings—those which take us out of ourselves, out of our minds, and out of control. As Shelley writes in *Prometheus Unbound,*

> The joy, the triumph, the delight, the madness!
> The boundless, overflowing, bursting gladness,
> The vaporous exultation not to be confined!
> Ha! Ha! The animation of delight
> Which wraps me, like an atmosphere of light,
> And bears me as a cloud is borne by its own wind.

Shelley finds madness attractive; it excites him. I suppose even Shelley was not mad enough to practice madness continuously in every dimension of life, but madness does not easily compartmentalize; it leaks through the walls from one compartment to another. Committed romantics understand this. Weekend romantics think that they can abandon themselves to promiscuity and dissipation and yet somehow wind up with a good job, a stable family life, and the man or woman of their dreams.

Second comes TRANSGRESSIVISM, the cult of forbidden feelings. The same fascination with morbidity which appears in Edgar Allen Poe appears in the homosexual movement, the Goth cult, the Dungeons and Dragons game, the fashions of the late Gianni Versace, and the philosophy of Friedrich Nietzsche. C. S. Lewis remarked in *That Hideous Strength,* "It is idle to point out to the perverted man the horror of his perversion: while the fierce fit is on, that horror is the very spice of his craving. It is ugliness itself that becomes, in the end, the goal of his lechery; beauty has long since grown too weak a stimulant. . . . [T]he terrible fascination suck[s] and tug[s] and fascinate[s] . . . [it is a] movement opposite to Nature . . . [an] impulse to reverse all reluctances and to draw every circle counter-clockwise."[8] This inversion of values is where all romantics will arrive if they follow the romantic path to the end. If the feeling you crave comes from crossing normal boundaries, then eventually you will have to cross the boundaries of normal feeling.

In third place is DETERMINISM, the cult of irresistable feelings, in which we consider ourselves merely catspaws of genes, or hormones, or neural circuitry, and declare in an unintended parody of Martin Luther, "So I feel; I can do no other." The attitude gives us an excuse for whatever we want to do, for "I can't help how I *feel,* and I *feel* I have no choice." In the defense is Steven Pinker, an evolutionary psychologist who writes of two young women who killed their newborns. The college girl left her dead child in a hotel dumpster with fractures to the skull; the college-bound girl delivered her child in a toilet stall, strangled him, stuffed him in a garbage can, then returned to the prom. Pinker says only that "The laws of biology were not kind" to these young mothers. Because of the way that the "emotional circuitry" of women has evolved in an "unforgiving world," mothers naturally kill babies who are born at the wrong time. How does he describe their state of mind? They "*feel* they [have] no choice."[9]

Fourth comes the CULT OF PLEASANT FEELINGS, called hedonism or utilitarianism according to whether one pursues pleasure for himself or for the group. Hedonistic themes are immensely successful in advertising, as in the following ad for Nike running shoes: "We are Hedonists and we want what feels good. We are all basically Hedonists. That's what makes us human. And we were made to want pretty simple things: Food. Water. Shelter. Warmth. And pleasure. We want what feels good. ... If it feels good then just do it." The philosophical versions of hedonism and utilitarianism aim at net pleasure rather than the pleasure of the moment, so they forgo some pleasures for fear of the associated pains. Epicurus, the most civilized hedonist, is said to have lived a quiet life. But this doesn't mean that the morality of pleasant feelings is safe. Consider the utilitarian Peter Singer, mentioned earlier, who thinks sick newborns should be killed because they cost society more pleasure than they give. They don't feel much anyway, he thinks.

Number five in our bestiary is AESTHETICISM, the worship of higher feelings. John Stuart Mill considered himself a utilitarian, but he recognized the flatheadedness of any philosophy that was unable to tell the difference between the pleasure of a pig cooling off in the mud and the pleasure of Socrates hot on the trail of the true, the good, and the beautiful. In the end he decided that some pleasures are higher than others, and the disparity is not merely quantitative, but qualitative. It isn't just a difference in amount, as though one viewing of Vermeer's *The Lacemaker* were better than two enjoyments of a hot fudge sundae, but one more sundae would tip the scales. No, just one glimpse of the Vermeer is worth the sacrifice of galaxies of sundaes. But the philosophy that Mill embraced is as terrible as the one that he rejected. If he was not a monster, it is only because his age took nothing to its conclusions. Ours takes everything to its conclusions. If the morality of pleasant feelings ends with Peter Singer, who thinks little humans may be killed because their pleasures aren't great enough, then the morality of higher feelings ends with Hannibal Lecter, who thinks vulgar humans may be killed because their pleasures aren't refined enough.[10]

The sixth variation on the cult of feelings is the adoration of religious feelings, or SPIRITUALISM. One form is the naïve exaltation of religious feelings as the voice of God—but exalting religious feelings, to exalting feelings as religious, is a shorter step than we realize. It was Keats who gave classic form to the latter notion: "I am certain of nothing but of the holiness of the Heart's affections and the truth of Imagination. . . . I have the same idea of all our passions as of love: they are all, in their sublime, creative of essential beauty."[11] Plainly he attributes to "affections," that is, to feelings, the attributes of holiness and creative power which belongs to God alone. The pop culture form of the notion is epitomized by the New Age writer Neale Donald Walsch, who quotes God as telling him "Mine is always your Highest Thought, your Clearest Word, your Grandest Feeling." A little later God tells him "The Grandest Feeling is that feeling which you call love." Still later God tells him love is not a particular feeling but "the summation of all feeling." The key is on the page where God tells him "My purpose for you is that you should know yourself as Me." There is a lot more of this faddle, but the meaning is clear. Whatever you feel, that is holy, because you are God, and God lives in what He feels.[12]

Seventh and last is the cult of *moral* feelings, or MORALISM. Head and shoulders above the other feeling cults, yet it too is fatally flawed. Its most eminent defender, James Q. Wilson, identifies the four main moral feelings as sympathy, duty, self-control, and fairness. He means by them pretty much what the rest of us do; the only puzzle is why he insists upon viewing them as feelings. For example he defines duty as "the disposition to honor obligations even without hope of reward or fear of punishment"[13]—but dispositions are not feelings but ways of acting, and obligations are not feelings but objective duties. He defines self-control as the ability to defer the "immediate and tangible" for the sake of the "future and uncertain,"[14] but surely the ability to resist one's feelings is not a feeling. In the end the morality of moral feelings turns out to be an attempt to represent an eyrie full of eagles as a goose. The rich palette of traditional ethics, with different colors for moral laws, moral virtues, moral feelings, and moral relationships, is stirred and blurred and mixed until but a single muddy color remains—moral feelings. Wilson's book is helpful for its abundant crosscultural data and its respect for common sense, but at times it reads a bit as though it were written in Orwell's Newspeak. The words that we need just aren't there.

I hope no one will accuse me of considering feelings unimportant. Our emotions give charm and energy to our lives, and even the inconvenient ones give information. The problem is that their charm is not self-evaluating, their energy is not self-directing, and their information is not self-interpreting. Virtue certainly includes feeling the right desires and emotions, but at the right times, toward the right people, and for the right reasons. Another way to view the problem is this. Our feelings are certainly a part of our inbuilt moral design. What the moralities of feelings try to do is make sense of the design in terms that are alien to design. Rather than asking what place feelings have in the big picture, they make feelings themselves the big picture. We should not be like the Stoics, sad men who took counsel with each other to rid their souls of feelings. But neither should we bow to our feelings as masters.

PART IV

RECOVERING THE LOST WORLD

Solzhenitsyn remarked that "the line dividing good and evil
cuts through the heart of every human being." So it does.
Even so, flawed people who oppose a culture of death
may challenge flawed people who support it.

9

The Public Relations
of Moral Wrong

*A closer look at how propaganda cannibalizes
moral knowledge and seduces moral sentiment.*

G. K. CHESTERTON REMARKED, "The modern world is insane, not so much because it admits the abnormal, as because it cannot recover the normal."[1] Is there any hope for the recovery of the normal? Yes, but first we must understand how the abnormal is popularized.

Whenever some new wrong takes root in society—divorce, lewdness, abortion, euthanasia, fetal experimentation, hatred of children, homosexual equivalence—we are told that it is part of a "new morality." There are two ways to think of this. According to the first view, there is a vast array of possible moralities, but only one of them is true; the task is to figure out which one it is. According to the second view, there is the same vast array of possible moralities, but *none* of them is true in itself; the significance of the one we choose is conferred merely by the fact that we choose it.

I will be expected to say that the former view is correct and that the latter is incorrect, but I must disappoint. Both views are false.

CANNIBALIZING CONSCIENCE

There is no vast array of possible moralities. Natural law is not the one true star in a galaxy of false ones; it is the only star. There is only one possible source of value judgments, one possible well from which moral duties can be drawn, one tree from which they can be plucked. The so-called new moralities do not pluck from different trees. They pluck from the same tree, but selectively.

The first writer to make the point explicitly, I believe, was C.S. Lewis. Drawn from the world conflicts of his day, his examples are illuminating. We are familiar with the communist "new morality" which made a fundamental duty of ending human need. Lewis quietly observes that the natural law agrees with Communists about the importance of feeding the hungry and clothing the naked. Unless the communist himself were drawing from the well of natural law, he could never have learned of such a duty. But side by side with it in the same well, and limiting it, are other duties, like fair play. The communist denies the limit, and uses one duty to debunk the others as bourgeois superstitions.

We are equally familiar with the fascist "new morality" which makes a fundamental duty of advancing one's own nation or people. However it may be perverted, the duty itself is real; "a duty to our own kin, because they are our own kin," lies deep in the storehouse of conscience, and there is no other place where it could have been found. But side by side with it in the same storehouse lies the stern duty of justice, which illuminates the special duty to kin by reminding us that in another way all men are kin. The fascist refuses the illumination.[2]

The strategy behind both of these examples is to select one moral precept, exaggerate its scope and importance, and use it as a club to beat down the others. But the lesson is broader than that. The foundational principles of right and wrong can be neither created nor destroyed by man; therefore, the only way to defeat the natural law is to make it cannibalize itself. Put another way, there are no new moralities, but only new perversions of the old one. This insight is crucial for understanding how the so-called new moralities are able to make us believe them. Moral error is a parasite on morality, and sucks all its plausibility from its host.

Now the natural law cannot really be turned against itself, because it is self-consistent: rightly understood, every moral principle is in harmony with every other. But with a little black magic, it can appear to oppose itself, and at least two different spells can be used to bring this appearance about.

The first spell is IMPOSTURE, which is using the perversion of a moral principle in place of the principle itself. Of course it is impossible for an imposter principle to satisfy conscience as well as the real thing does, so the real thing must first be weakened by misrepresentation. Consider marriage. Love is a permanent and unqualified commitment of the will to the true good of another. Now the only way to make a chain is to attach the links, and in similar fashion the only way to bind the will is to make a promise; there is no other way to do it. But because this particular promise is so difficult and so deeply important to the future of the community, it is performed before witnesses who pledge to do all in their power to hold the couple to their vows and help them live up to them. Such a ceremony can easily be misrepresented as a mere legalism for subduing the insincere. When this happens, people say that if they are really in love, they "don't need a piece of paper"—which really means that those who do make promises love less purely than those who don't, or that those who don't marry are more truly married than those who do. So it is that cohabitation, a violation of marital purity, is defended in the name of marriage itself; it becomes an *impostor* to the dignity of marriage.

The spell which Lewis had in mind was UNRAVELING, which is using the perversion of one moral principle against another. Like imposture, unraveling too requires misrepresentation of the principle attacked. Consider the movement to recognize homosexual liaisons as marriages.

The principle attacked is marital purity; the principle used against it is fairness; but the argument distorts both the meaning of the principle and the nature of the institution, so that morality seems to turn against itself. Here is how it works. Fairness is said to forbid treating people differently. That is a half-truth; what fairness actually forbids is *arbitrarily* treating people differently, as well as arbitrarily treating them the same. It would not serve the fairness of baseball to declare every score a tie, because the purpose of baseball involves competition. In the same way, the purpose of marriage involves procreation, and it does not serve its fairness to pretend that sodomy is anything but sterile. To call procreation the purpose of marriage is not arbitrary; alone among the forms of human union, the union of the sexes produces children, and if it were just another kind of friendship there would be no compelling reason to regulate it. A legislature can no more turn sodomitical unions into marriages than it can turn dogs into cats; it can only *unravel* the institution of marriage by sowing confusion about its purposes. So it is that the real moral duty of fairness is made to seem at war with the real moral duty of marital purity.

SEDUCING PARACONSCIENCE

So far I have discussed the public relations of moral wrong strictly in terms of conscience. But conscience, *as moral knowledge*, does not motivate all by itself. It has helpers—desires and emotions which might be called paraconscience.[3] Chief among these servants is the desire for the good, without which, obviously, the mere knowledge of the good would be inert. Among the many others are outrage, or indignation, the feeling which cooperates with the duty of justice by moving us to rectify and punish; pity, or compassion, the feeling which cooperates with the duty of lovingkindness by moving us to succor and relieve; and modesty, or shame, the feeling which cooperates with the duty of decorum by repelling us from the unseemly and indecent. Borrowing an image from Plato, the great and difficult achievement which we call "virtue" can be viewed as a cooperative relationship between paraconscience and conscience, in which conscience is the horseman who activates and directs the eagerness of the horse to run.

If the public relations of moral wrong are to succeed, then it is not enough to cannibalize conscience; one must also seduce paraconscience. If moral error derives its *plausibility* from the known moral truths which it distorts, then it derives its *power to motivate* from the emotions and desires which ought to be allied with moral truth but are pulled away.

How are they pulled away? The "trust your feelings" ideology which I discussed in the previous chapter is a big part of the story. If conscience is a horseman and paraconscience is the horse, then the effect of the feelings cult is to loosen the saddle and make the horse buck, so that the rider falls off and the horse runs away by itself. Of course the horse might run in the direction where the horseman would have guided it anyway. In a society with centuries of moral discipline behind it, that is exactly what tends to happen—for a while. Through what might be called emotional habit, people continue to feel like doing what is, in fact, their duty, even though they no longer think of it as their duty, and even though the glue which binds feeling to duty has dissolved. Unfortunately, if nothing reinforces the habit, eventually it follows the glue into oblivion.

But the "trust your feelings" ideology is not the *whole* of the story. Cultural revolutions are not accomplished merely by dissolving moral discipline so that feelings wander whithersoever they please. The emotions and desires must be redisciplined, rehabituated, so that—so much as possible—they go where the new riders want. Each argument from false principle must be matched with a motive from false feeling.

In our day, the seduction and redirection of the emotions and desires has achieved its greatest success with the feeling of compassion. In compassion we *feel with* the sufferer, but there is a right way and a wrong way to do this. One way relieves *his* suffering, the other relieves what I suffer for him; one gives him what he needs, the other merely gives him what he wants—or just puts him out of sight. Compassion ought to make us visit the prisoner, dry out the alcoholic, help the pregnant girl prepare for the baby, and encourage the young homosexual to live chastely. But how much easier it is to forget the prisoner, give the drunk a drink, send the girl to the abortionist, and tell the kid to just give in. False compassion is a great deal less work than true.

False compassion has other advantages too. It sits easier with our unrepented sins, for it is hard to tell the homosexual to live chastely if I try to get in bed with every attractive woman I meet. In the short run it causes me less conflict with other people, for I sympathize with whatever anyone may feel. It certainly requires less moral reflection, because I believe every sad story and give in to every tearful "I want." It fits in particularly well with the inclinations of teenagers, who are discovering sympathy for the first time, find it as intoxicating as catnip, and love to hear sad stories of the heartlessness of the grown-up world. If they have not had clear moral training, it even seems to them to resemble the Golden Rule. "If *I* got pregnant, I know *I* wouldn't want to have the baby; if *I* were gay, I know *I* wouldn't want anyone telling me I couldn't get married." This property makes false compassion especially useful for corrupting the minds of the very young, stuffing them with false wisdom before the true wisdom has time to develop.

But any element of paraconscience can be seduced. It makes no difference how noble a particular desire or passion may seem to be; the nobler it is in itself, the baser it will be if corrupted. Only Good was created. Every evil thing is a good thing ruined. There are no other ways to get one.

DOUBLING THE SCRIPT

The public relations of moral wrong inevitably require two different scripts, two different versions of the justifying story: One for the shock troops of the movement, another for the people outside it. Each script employs different arguments. In the public script, certain subjects are avoided altogether:

> *Senator Boxer:* I will answer the question [about] when the baby is born. The baby is born when the baby is outside the mother's body. The baby is born.
>
> *Senator Santorum:* I am not going to put words in your mouth—
>
> *Senator Boxer:* I hope not.
>
> *Senator Santorum:* But, again, what you are suggesting is if the baby's toe is inside the mother, you can, in fact, kill that baby.
>
> *Senator Boxer:* Absolutely not.
>
> *Senator Santorum:* OK. So if the baby's toe is in, you can't kill the baby. How about if the baby's foot is in?
>
> *Senator Boxer:* You are the one who is making these statements.
>
> *Senator Santorum:* We are trying to draw a line here.
>
> *Senator Boxer:* I am not answering these questions.[4]

Some such doubling of the script takes place in every movement for moral wrong, not just in totalitarian regimes but in stained republics like our own. Corrupted journalists play along, doing all in their power to keep outsiders from learning how the insiders think. Watch the coverage of a homosexual rights parade. The camera lingers on the pretty girl walking cheerfully with her parents; somehow it misses the marchers for the North American Man-Boy Love Association, right behind. Or consider the public rhetoric of the abortion movement. Neither life nor death is mentioned, but only that vaguest of abstractions, "choice"; yet just offstage the insiders are talking about how the fetus is "objectively at fault for causing pregnancy"[5] and how "a woman who gives life may also destroy life" in a "new allocation of life and death powers."[6]

The reasons for the difference between the insider script and the public script are fairly plain. The first is that, driven by the Furies, the shock troops of a movement for moral evil have different psychological needs. After they have plundered the palace of moral knowledge for material wherewith to build allurements to the evil they promote, they must go back into the palace and ransack it all over again—this time for sacrifices to appease an avenging conscience. The second reason is that it would be imprudent to discuss such dread sacrifices in front of outsiders. The details would shock and repel them, not draw them in. Immoralist movements require converts, or at least fellow travellers.

It is amazing that we are not more familiar with the phenomenon of the double script, because it has occurred in every great historical movement of moral evil. Consider the Holocaust. Only a small number of Germans belonged to the inner core of the Nazi movement. Although the non-Jewish population was asked to support the removal of the Jews to remote locations, they were never asked to support the extermination campaign itself; if ordinary people didn't ask too many questions, that was enough. The Nazis themselves wanted to kill Jews, of course, but even the would-be executioners knew that human life is sacred. Therefore they could not *just* slaughter their victims; somehow they had to explain it to themselves. One way was to cannibalize the principle of retributive justice. The Jews were evil, so the story ran, therefore they deserved to be punished. Injustice drew force from distortion of the precept of justice. In some measure it must have felt *right* to kill.

But not right enough. After all, the extermination program was nothing like ordinary capital punishment. There were no trials, the methods were brutal, and the ss could hardly have failed to realize that few of their victims were guilty of any sort of crime. Even small children beneath the age of reason were being killed. Notwithstanding the rationalization that Jews deserved what they got, guilty knowledge was an overwhelming burden for the exterminators. Robert Jay Lifton reports on an interview with a former *Wehrmacht* neuropsychiatrist who had treated large numbers of death camp soldiers for psychological disorders. Their symptoms were much like those of combat troops, but they were worse and lasted longer. The men had the hardest time shooting women and children, especially children, and many of them had nightmares of punishment or retribution.[7] And so the knowledge of the sacredness of human life had to be further appeased. Jews and other prisoners had to be made to seem not just more evil, but *less human.*

In the idea of the *untermensch* or underman, propaganda had long fused these two themes. One ss pamphlet contended, "from a biological point of view he seems completely normal. He has hands and feet and a sort of brain. But, in fact, he is a completely different creature, a horror. He only looks human, with a human face, but his spirit is lower than that of an animal. A terrible chaos runs rampant in this creature, an awful urge for destruction, primitive desires, unparalleled evil, a monster, subhuman."[8] But propaganda alone did not suffice. Measures had to be taken to humiliate the Jews before killing them, like herding them naked from the train disembarkation platform to the barracks. Gitta Sereny asked Franz Stangl, the former commandant of the Treblinka death camp, "If they were going to kill them anyway, what was the point of all the humiliation, why the cruelty?" He replied, "To condition those who actually had to carry out the policies. To make it possible for them to do what they did."[9]

Here we see the deepest reason for the double script. What would have happened if the general population had seen prisoners treated in these ways? Ordinary people would have been unlikely to conclude that the Jews were like animals; they would have concluded that the camp guards were. If only the explanation *were* as simple as Stangl told Sereny! That explanation was horrible enough; but the true explanation is more terrible still. For how could such a strategy as he described work even with the ss? How could they "forget" *who it was* that had reduced their prisoners to a subhuman appearance? If they had not been so guilty already, surely they couldn't have; because they were guilty, they had to. They had to "forget" because they had worse things to "forget," and this was the only way to forget them. Crushed between the millstones of inward accusation, the minds of the soldiers declared that anyone they could treat so inhumanely *couldn't* be human. It was unthinkable. Wrong thus became self-justifying.

The same thing happens on a smaller scale every day. A man participates in some wrong. Not because of shamelessness but shame, he turns activist; he crusades for it. Imagine what it must really be like inside an abortion facility. Picture the operator piecing the body parts back together after a D&E to make sure they are all there—two arms, two legs, one torso, one head. Before a meeting of fellow abortionists, Warren Hern and Billie Corrigan, a physician and nurse, respectively, describe a survey of fifteen of Hern's present and former staff. Some of the staff report that they refuse to look at the fetus. Others look, but feel "shock, dismay, amazement, disgust, fear, and sadness." Two thought that the abortion "must eventually damage the physician psychologically." One found herself becoming increasingly resentful about the casual attitudes of some patients, even though she approved of abortion herself. Two of the staff described dreams of vomiting up fetuses, or about protecting other people from looking at them.[10]

"We discerned," write the authors, "that the following psychological defenses were used by staff members at various times to handle the traumatic impact of the destructive part of the operation: denial, sometimes shown by the distance a person keeps from viewing D&E; projection, shown by excessive concern or anguish for other staff members assisting with or performing D&E ; and rationalization." They conclude,

> Some part of our cultural and perhaps even biological heritage recoils at a destructive operation on a form that is similar to our own, even though we know that the act has a positive effect for a living person. No one who has not performed D & E can know what it is

like or what it means; but having performed it, we are bewildered by the possibilities of interpretation."

We have reached a point in this particular technology where there is no possibility of denying an act of destruction. It is before one's eyes. The sensations of dismemberment flow through the forceps like an electric current. It is the crucible of a raging controversy, the confrontation of a modern existential dilemma. The more we seem to solve the problem, the more intractable it becomes.[11]

No wonder the script must be doubled.

SEVEN DEGREES OF DESCENT

The doubling of the script is an evasion, but not just an evasion. Inevitably, the public relations of moral wrong require lies, and a lot of them. What we call "honest mistakes" can only go so far. There are the lies about whether infidelity and promiscuity really hurt anyone. There are the lies about whether the living child is really alive, or really a child. Next come lies about the meaning of fairness, the nature of promises, and what the "committed gay relationship" is really like. Amid all of them is the lie about how hard it is to know what to do.

Professional advocates for the so-called new moralities are specialists in such mendacity, and debate with such an advocate is not an edifying experience. At a critical point, he makes a statement which flatly reverses the truth, in an area where he is too well-informed to be mistaken. He knows he is lying. You know he is lying. He knows you know it. You know he knows you do. But both of you know that the audience does not know, and so he lies on. His is the advantage, because the average falsehood takes only five seconds to utter but a hundred and fifty to explode. A sound bite lasts only ten.

The foulness of it all brings to mind a question put to me long ago by one of my teachers. "Don't you think there is more lying in politics

than there used to be?" he asked. "Why do you think that this is happening?" At the time, young oaf that I was, I thought his question silly,
but I have come to think better of it. Our public people do lie more,
and for the same reasons that most of us lie more. More's the pity, the
more we lie the more easily we are taken in by their lies. There are seven
degrees of descent on the downward staircase of honesty. Not all of us
are at the bottom, but most of us are at a lower stair than we admit.

The first and topmost stair is simply SIN. The greater our trespasses,
the more we have to lie about. We lie about money, sex, and our children, because we sin about money, sex, and our children. A turning point
in both public and private life came in the early seventies, when we legalized the private use of lethal violence against babies yet unborn. The
justification of such staggering betrayal takes more lies than there are
words to tell them.

The second stair is SELF-PROTECTION. Lies are weaklings; they need
bodyguards. Even the smallest prevarication needs a ring of perjuries
to keep from being seen. But each new lie needs its own protective ring.
Pretty soon the liar is smothered in layers of mendacity, as numerous as
onion shells, as thick as flannel blankets.

Third down is HABITUATION. We make habits of everything; it is
part of our nature. Courage and magnanimity become habits, and so
does the chewing of gum. In time lying too becomes a habit. After you
have lied awhile for need, you begin to lie without need. It becomes
second nature. You hardly notice that you do it. Asked why, you can give
no reason. You have crossed the border between lying and being a liar.

Underneath the previous stair is SELF-DECEPTION, for beyond a certain point, a person starts losing track of truth. Your heart cannot bear
to believe that you lie as hugely as you do, so to relieve the rubbing, itch-
ing, pricking needles of rue, you half-believe your own lies.

RATIONALIZATION follows next in order. As your grasp on the truth
continues to weaken, you come to blame its weakness on truth itself.
It's so slippery, so elusive, who can hold it? It changes shape, moves

around, just won't sit still. Not at all fair of it, but everything is shades of gray anyway. How silly to believe in absolutes. Truth is what we let each other get away with, that's all.

Sixth comes TECHNIQUE. Lying becomes a craft. For example, you discover that a great falsehood repeated over and over works even better than a small one. Nobody can believe that you would tell such a whopper; therefore, you have a motive to make every lie a whopper. This technique, called the Big Lie after a remark in Hitler's *Mein Kampf*,[12] is not a monopoly of dictators, or even of politicians; probably no one uses it in public life before he has practiced it in private. Our American variation on the Big Lie works by numbers instead of size. If you lie about everything, no matter how small, nobody can believe you would tell so *many* lies. The whistleblowers exhaust themselves trying to keep up with you, and eventually they have blown their whistles so many times that people think *they* must be the liars. By the time a few of your lies are found out, the virtue of honesty has become so discredited that no one cares whether you are lying or not. "They all do it."

The seventh and bottommost stair is that DUTY TURNS UPSIDE-DOWN. Why does this happen? Because the moment lying is accepted instead of condemned, it has to be required. If it is just another way to win, then in refusing to lie for the cause or the company, you aren't doing your job.

This is where we are, and this is who we are becoming. The problem is not just in our politicians, for they came from us and we elected them. It is not just in the shock troops of evil, for we have made room in the big tent for them. Do we dare at last yield ourselves to Truth, to be scraped, scoured and made honest until we can give back His light?

10

The Public Relations
of Moral Right

*"Right reason" is still achievable, though
it does not come easily to fallen nature.*

To RELIEVE THE STING OF GUILT, we entomb it in nacre until it seems beautiful to us. For that and all the other reasons in this book, every movement to excuse a moral wrong becomes a movement to condone it, and every movement to condone a moral wrong becomes a movement to extend it. In struggling against everyday sickness, sorrow, and crime we struggle against particular evils; there are no pro-sickness, pro-sorrow, or pro-crime *movements*. There are, however, *immoralist* movements, and in struggling against the immoralist movements of the day we struggle against evil as such.

THE NATURE OF THE CONFLICT

The previous chapter described the public relations of moral wrong as "black magic." Their methods do not require eye of newt, but they might as well: In essence, they are forms of *goeteia,* of the ancient practice whose goal was to acquire power by "breaking" nature, unpatterning its patterns, uncreating creation. The homosexual movement ultimately seeks not the protection of homosexuals from cruelty, but the annihilation of natural boundaries. The euthanasia movement ultimately seeks not an end to pain, but endless death. The cloning project ultimately seeks not a solution to childlessness, but the confusion of human identity. The eugenics project ultimately seeks not a cure of disease, but the overthrow of the Creator by the creature. The latter two movements barely register as yet in public consciousness, as the former two barely registered a scant generation ago. But they are the *goeteia* of the future.

So soon as it makes peace with basic evil, even a movement for a good end becomes evil. Consider the fate of feminism. Whatever the strengths or weaknesses of its philosophy may have been, the nineteenth-century feminism was substantially what it claimed to be: An effort to protect women from mistreatment, and to secure for them a wider sphere of opportunity. It never tried to separate the interest of the mother from the interest of the child, and it recognized that there was nothing "pro-woman" about the killing of an infant in the womb. Susan B. Anthony called abortion "child murder" and wrote this about it: "Guilty? Yes. No matter what the motive, love of ease, or a desire to save from suffering the unborn innocent, the woman is awfully guilty who commits the deed. It will burden her conscience in life, it will burden her soul in death; But oh! Thrice guilty is he who drove her to the desperation which impelled her to the crime!"[1]

But from the day that feminism embraced this creeping malevolence, it was doomed. All its good intentions were inverted, and the real purpose of the movement quickly became the defamation of everything distinctive about female human nature: especially the destruction of the relationship between the mother and the child. Feminist Eileen L. McDonagh calls the unborn child a "private party" who "coerces" the woman "to be pregnant against her will"; it "becomes the master of her body and her liberty, putting her in the position of its slave." She has a "right to consent to a relationship with this intruder," and is "entitled to use deadly force to stop it," even if it "acquires the highly charged label of 'baby.'" "Baby" is not a natural category, "dictated by the essence of things" but a conventional way of speaking, "established by our decision." When a student tells her that "Pregnancy is having a living person inside of you"—which would seem to be literally true—she says this is only a "loosely constructed metaphor" which is "culturally derived." There you have the essence of *goeteia*. There is no nature; there are no *givens*; reality is to be what we decide. Black magic.[2]

So the first necessity of the public relations of moral right is to recognize the nature of the conflict. The immoralist movements are not isolated phenomena, but branches of the goetic arts; they are united in their hatred of the human design, and, by extension, of its Designer. The second necessity is to abstain from the polluted languages of goetic incantation. The abortion movement is not about choice, but about death. The feminist movement is not for mothers, but against them. The homosexual movement is not gay, but whistling in the graveyard. The Brave New World of cloning and fetal tissue research is not about healing, but about playing God.

There is no virtue in giving offense, but there is a difference between avoidable and unavoidable offense. To fail to avoid the avoidable kind is the vice of scandal. To try to avoid the unavoidable kind is the vice of complicity in evil.

PERMANENT ADVANTAGES OF GOOD AND EVIL

As the web-weavers of *goeteia* twine ever new word-tangles of confusion, ever changing ways to rationalize, it is necessary to find ever new ways to explain old truth. In one way this is like an arms race: as each side adds new weapons to its arsenal, the other side tries to counter. In another way it is different from an arms race: the assumption of equivalence fails to hold. Each side has certain permanent advantages in resources, and certain permanent disadvantages as well. When I say "permanent," I mean as to the duration of this world.

To the permanent advantage of evil is that it can rationalize. To its permanent disadvantage is that it must. To its further advantage is the fact that the ordinary people who oppose it are equally tempted to make nests for their sins in the spreading branches of moral law. But to its further disadvantage is this: that the ordinary people it ensnares are equally loved by God, and cannot by any magic but free will be placed beyond the possibility of redemption.

Those who seek the good have a permanent advantage in the ultimately inescapable human moral design. They have a greater advantage in the indestructibility of that part of the design called deep conscience, which, like a signal buoy, keeps rising. And they have an illimitable advantage in the Designer Himself, who is not a remote intelligence but a God who hears their prayers, cannot be defeated or caught by surprise, and acts beyond apparent defeats in ways they do not see.

Perhaps their greatest permanent disadvantage is that through the sheer horror of devastation, their opponents can tempt them to despair. This is a burden. But they have a permanent advantage in the virtue St. Paul calls hope, for their confidence, unlike the bravado of their opponents, is not presumption; it does not rest in their own small strength, but in the strength of the one whom they serve. I am reminded of a debate in which the pro-abortion speaker grew impatient. "Don't you people understand that you've lost?" she demanded. "The fat lady has sung." Her opponent replied, "It's not over when the fat lady sings but when the angel blows his horn."

This sort of thing will not get into any course on rhetoric; it is not about tropes and forms of argument. But there are things to be said about those important matters also, and to them we now turn.

WHAT TO AVOID

Cultural activists tend to fall into four common mistakes when defending the natural law in the public square. These might be called exclusivism, pearl casting, conversionism, and accommodationism. I give particular attention to the members of my faith, among whom several of these errors are especially common.

Exclusivism. The exclusivist approach to engaging the broader culture can be expressed in a single word: *Don't.* Exclusivists preach to the choir. Although they may speak in public settings where people who do not share their assumptions are present, they ignore them, pitching their appeal to those who agree with them, sounding just those chords to which they can expect their allies to respond. Although it may be surprising that anyone interested in recovering a sane moral culture would follow such an approach, exclusivism does have a selling point: Though it can never build a *broad* movement because it alienates potential allies, it can build an *enthusiastic* movement because it activates the "base," the true believers. In arenas where small numbers make big differences, for example political party caucuses, such enthusiasts may even achieve their short-term goals, which makes exclusivism a difficult mistake to unlearn. Nevertheless it is a mistake. Although it might carve a presence in a political party, it cannot change the culture. Although it would no doubt activate a "moral" majority if such a thing existed, it cannot build one where it does not exist already. Moreover it arouses the other side's true believers at least as much as it arouses its own. Exclusivism is probably an important reason for the paradox of the "Religious Right," expressed in the remark of conservative activist Paul Weyrich that "we got our people elected. But that did not result in the adoption of our agenda."[3]

Pearl casting. The difference between pearl casters and exclusivists is that while exclusivists are *trying* to preach to the choir, pearl casters do it without meaning to. Their approach to cultural engagement is to hit people over the head with their sacred texts. Naïvely, they assume that their neighbors are interested in these authorities, and sincerely believe that their method of conversation is a good way to persuade the unpersuaded. This is the tactic of those well-meaning legions who write letters to their local newspapers, endlessly and uselessly repeating "the Bible says." Variations include "The Pope says," "Talmud says"—even "the natural law tradition says," for an appeal to what we *can't not know* is not the same as an appeal to a tradition we might never have heard of. To be sure, all these authorities affirm the norms built into our created nature, and there are appropriate times to quote all of them in the public square. But one must first cultivate the willingness of the audience to hear them. Among my own co-religionists, the form of pearl casting which hits people over the head with the Bible is sometimes called "biblicism." Let it be said, however, that endless quotation from the Bible is the opposite of the Bible's model for speaking to the unconvinced. When addressing pagans, the apostles always began with what the listeners knew and believed already. If a sharper argument is needed, there is a "hard saying" in the gospels about not casting pearls before creatures who wallow in mud, lest they trample them underfoot and then turn to attack. If the metaphor seems harsh, one should try pitching Bible verses at a press conference, and see what happens.

Conversionism. The conversionist solution to these difficulties is to proselytize. Among fundamentalist Christians, it takes the form "Just bring people to Christ; He will take care of the rest."[4] If only everyone were converted, they reason, there wouldn't be any more cultural problems, so evangelism becomes the only legitimate means of cultural engagement. A Christian myself, I believe in evangelism, but it is not a means of cultural engagement at all. In the first place one can become a Christian without developing a Christian view of created reality. The texts of Christianity itself attest this fact; Paul *exhorts* believers to "be transformed by the renewing of your mind"[5] rather than merely assuming that they are. Conversionism is attended by two other difficulties as well. One is that it is unrealistic (and most unbiblical) to expect everyone to be converted. The other is that a measure of good will can be found even outside the community of faith. This too is biblical. There was Pharaoh; but there was also Cyrus.[6]

Accommodationism. Accommodationists seek to change not people's minds, but their momentary behavior, by tailoring their message to the desires and opinions of whoever they are talking to at the time. "I know you don't agree with me about this, but it's good from your perspective too. Here's what's in it for you." Insofar as not everything which other people seek or think is bad, there is a grain of merit in this approach, but it fails to distinguish between what can be affirmed and what cannot be affirmed. Just as there are some groups with which it can never be right to ally, there are some interests to which it can never be right to appeal, like malice, revenge, or racism.

WHAT TO DO

Superficially, the classical approach to cultural engagement resembles the accommodationist approach because it appeals to people in terms of what they already believe. The differences, however, are great. In the first place, classical persuaders appeal not to *whatever* people already believe, but to the scattered points of truth in what they believe. Because of the Four Witnesses, one can always expect to find some; the task is to connect the dots. In the second place, classical persuaders are real persuaders, not pseudo-persuaders; their aim is to change minds, not just behavior. The method is the same whether one is defending the purity of marriage, pleading the sanctity of life, or soliciting respect for the genome. One begins with what people know or intuit already, and one builds on it.

Several years ago I had the honor of hearing one of the world's most distinguished scholars of natural law expound the nature of the basic good of marriage. Considering the times, a great portion of his lecture had to be devoted to why marriage is intrinsically heterosexual. The talk was perfectly logical, but to most people it would have seemed esoteric.

During the discussion period, therefore, I asked him how he would make the case to ordinary people. He seemed surprised; apparently thinking that I was confused and was referring to myself, he summarized. I clarified my question. The request I set for him was not to repeat the case for marriage that he had just made to us, but to explain how he would make the case for marriage in the public square. Now he understood what I was asking. He thought for a little while, and then he said, "I think it makes its own case."

Exactly. And that is the classical approach. One cannot convince people of what they grasp already; one can only draw it out of them. When the citizens of California voted on a whether the traditional understanding of marriage should be preserved or discarded, the homosexual lobby pulled out all the stops: restricting marriage to a man and a woman is unjust, it lacks compassion, and so forth. Underfunded, the defenders of the traditional understanding focussed on a few television spots showing families with children, enjoying everyday activities familiar to everyone. It was heartening that television was put to an ethical use for a change. The images reminded people that marriage is a procreative partnership, the foundation of the family, a precious good worth preserving against distortion. Sodomy *cannot* ground families; it is sterile in every sense of the term.

No doubt both sides engaged pricey consultants and showed their ads to "focus groups" first. What interests a natural law thinker, however, is that the pro-marriage ads appealed to a universal human good, to a theme one would expect to resonate with "focus groups" in all times, all places, all civilizations. They made use, in other words, of the permanent natural advantages of the good. For the other side—even in a culture as confused as ours—this was impossible. The appeal to false justice and false compassion could never have the power of the appeal to real family.

Some thinkers affirm the natural law *in principle,* but reject the classical approach. They do not deny the obviousness of the moral facts, but they believe that fallen man is constitutionally incapable of admitting the obvious. We can try to find common ground, they say, but once we reach our neighbor's deepest assumptions—the bottommost presuppositions of his world-view—we are stuck. There is no way to challenge these deepest assumptions, because he recognizes nothing deeper in the name of which we can challenge them. Appealing to the Four Witnesses is fruitless; all we can do is show him that his assumptions are in conflict with each other, as inevitably they will be. The idea is that the moment he realizes the conflict among his assumptions, he is in crisis; he must either try to hold onto his worldview, *knowing that it is incoherent,* or embrace another one which will inevitably have the same problem. When every intellectual refuge has been destroyed, one by one, then finally he may be ready to embrace a sane view of moral reality. Sometimes this approach to persuasion is called "presuppositional."

But in the radical form in which I have summarized it, the presuppositional approach is incoherent too. It raises questions which, by its own lights, it cannot answer. In the first place, *why* must every worldview opposed to the natural law be incoherent? It may be false, but that is not the same thing; nothing prevents a set of assumptions from being false and yet mutually compatible. In the second place, if fallen man really is incapable of admitting the obvious, then why should he *care* whether his worldview is incoherent? Why should he even admit the principle of non-contradiction? Nothing is more common among postmodern folk than to deny it; they tell themselves reality itself is incoherent. The upshot is that persuasion should be impossible. Communication should be impossible. Every worldview should be sealed unto itself, with no door in and no door out. The worldview of natural law should be no different, in this respect, than any of the rest.

A more sensible view is that reality poses a constant problem for fallen man. He wants to acknowledge some of the truth which presses in on him, but taken together it points too strongly to other truth which he resists with all his might. In the end, he must deny so many obvious things that the work is just too much. He is like a man in a bathtub, surrounded by dozens of corks, trying to hold all of them down at once. Whenever he pushes one down, another somewhere else pops right back up. This is the reason why his worldview is inevitably incoherent, for bits of truth get into it that he does not intend, clashing with the things he does intend. In most cases, one of these bits is the principle of non-contradiction. That is why the incoherence of his worldview bothers him, and that, in turn, is why one may get somewhere by pointing out this incoherence to him.

It follows from what has been said that when a presuppositional approach to persuasion works at all, what enables it to work is the flotsam of natural law—all those corks of truth that can't all be kept down at once. But calling attention to the corks is the keystone of the classical approach to persuasion, so moderate presuppositionalism turns out to be just one of its variations. Pursued to the exclusion of other variations, it would be most unwise; but it is sometimes useful in talking with people who are deep behind the brickwork of denial.

A good example of how the corks keep popping up is found in the pro-abortion writer from whom I quoted a few pages earlier. Feminist McDonagh would have us regard the unborn child as an aggressor. Yet even she cannot deny that this is not how mothers normally view their gestation. She tries to have it both it both ways: "The view of pregnancy as a form of intrusive aggression against a woman by a fertilized ovum does not preclude other depictions of pregnancy as a symbiotic union of mother and child. No species would survive if mothers viewed offspring solely as aggressors. The key word here is *solely*. The view of pregnancy as intrusive aggression by a fetus does not substitute for all other views but rather expands the continuum of legal and social constructions of pregnancy so that it, too, has the same latitude as other intimate relationships, such as sexual intercourse."[7] Again, "Since pregnancy, like all intimate experiences, means many things, for one of the meanings to involve the fetus as an aggressor does not rob pregnancy of its many other positive meanings."[8]

But of course this is utterly absurd. Viewing pregnancy as aggression against the mother by the child *does* exclude viewing it as the nurture of the child by the mother, and McDonagh, a lawyer, wants only the former view to be recognized in law. Would one get anywhere by pointing out to her that she wants to have her cake and eat it too? The chances are small; professional advocates of moral wrong are deeply vested in not seeing things like that. But could one get anywhere by going over her head and pointing it out to young minds she may wish to seduce? That is much more promising.

COUNTERMEASURES

In the previous chapter we considered three techniques in the public relations of moral wrong: Cannibalizing conscience, seducing paraconscience, and doubling the script. What are the countermeasures? We will consider them in reverse order, last first.

The countermeasure to the doubling of the script is reuniting it. Certain international sponsors of terrorism have made a fine art of saying "Peace, peace" to the Western press in English, but saying "War, war" to their domestic constituencies in their own languages. The fitting response (which, for reasons best known to themselves, few in the Western press employ) is to make a routine practice of publishing the English statements side by side with translations of the foreign-language statements, so that Western citizens can compare them for themselves. Nothing prevents the use of the same countermeasure when our own immoralists double the script. Although what they say among themselves is not circulated to the general public, neither is it secret; it certainly *can* be circulated to the general public. For example, do abortion proponents publicly deny their enmity to motherhood? Publicize Eileen L. McDonagh's portrayal of the unborn baby as an intrusive aggressor who is guilty of causing pregnancy. Do homosexual activists publicly deny the connection between homosexuality and pedophilia? Publicize the double issue of the *Journal of Homosexuality* on the topic of "Male Intergenerational Love," packed with articles in praise of the "loving pedophile."[9] It might be said that every social movement has embarrassing allies. Quite so, but there is a fundamental asymmetry. Decent social movements repudiate would-be friends who say foul things. Immoralist movements take them to their breasts because they do not regard the things they say as foul. This speaks loudly, if only we have ears.

The countermeasure to the seduction of paraconscience is to woo it back. Have people been taken in by false compassion? Then show true compassion. A supreme illustration is the daily work of crisis pregnancy centers, where women, sometimes in gravest distress, are able to speak with other women, volunteers, who have no financial stake in the exploitation of their misery and seek only to show them love. At no cost, the centers offer services like pregnancy testing, medical referral, information about abortion and adoption, lifestyle counseling, long-term mentoring, clothing and supplies for both mothers and babies, church and social service referral, childbirth classes, parenting classes, help in family reconciliation, and post-abortion counseling groups. For all these mercies, they suffer canards—"they only care about the fetus, not the mother," "as soon as the baby is born, they forget about him," "they tell women not to abort, but offer them no support." Pro-abortion organizations regularly sent them *agents provocateurs* who pretend to seek help but whose aim is to incite counselors into speaking or behaving inappropriately. So desperate is iniquity to be justified! Yet the quiet tenderness of crisis pregnancy centers has probably had more influence on what ordinary people think about abortion than all that has been written on the subject, and their model of personal and sacrificial love puts the mass-produced "compassion" of the state's social service delivery systems to shame.

Challenging false compassion comes especially hard for public officials. One does not win elections by saying "No," and the first impulse of a legislator who is accused of being "mean" is to change the subject.

I have a dream that some day, some statesman will blaze another path, saying something in his speeches like this:

> I know that many of you women listening to me have had abortions yourselves. That is just why I think I can level with you: You, more than anyone, know what abortion means. Some people would have you believe that to call for an end to abortion is to be cold, unfeeling, uncompassionate. They would have you believe that the kindest thing you can do for a woman in a crisis pregnancy is to put her in the hands of an abortionist, to do what abortionists do. But those people have not sat up with you and wept for the child that might have been. Those people have not listened with you in the stillness of the night, waiting, like you, to hear the echo of a dream of a cry of a baby that you will never hold. Those people have not heard you ask in the secrecy of your thoughts, "What if?"
>
> You are not the same woman, please God, that you were when you listened to those people years ago. From your own regret, you know now that they were wrong. Sometimes the grief is just a whisper, sometimes it is as keen as a knife; but it is never far. I ask you to have the moral courage to reflect on your experience. I ask you to gather up the mercy to spare others the knife in your heart. I ask you to make a world in which no one's daughter will be tempted, as you were, by the false promise of an easy "solution" which only brings more pain than before. There will always be reasons for broken hearts; but for all our children, *that* reason, perhaps, we can end.

That would be a statesman indeed, for he would have to lash himself to the mast like Odysseus, deafening his ears to the siren songs of his political advisors. To improve the comparison: not like Odysseus, but like Lincoln.

At last we come to the cannibalizing of conscience, of moral knowledge. What is the countermeasure here? When someone has been taken in by a sophistical argument which makes an apparent moral necessity of moral wrong—how is it possible to respond? The one thing needful is to distinguish between those who are honestly confused, and those who would only like to think that they are.

The honestly confused rarely need more than reminders and simple clarifications: reminders of the moral principles which have been shoved aside, clarifications of the ones which have been distorted. This is far less difficult than academics like me make it out to be. If we are talking about what "commitments" are, anyone can see the difference between promising and not promising. If we are discussing what "fairness" means, it is hardly beyond the capacity of plain people to see that arbitrarily treating people differently is not the same as treating people differently for a reason. Although there are a few hard cases in ethics, the overpowering majority of everyday moral decisions are not hard, but easy; and yet these are where people become confused.

The main reason it seems so difficult to clear up honest moral confusion is that most moral confusion is not honest. People do not fall into profound error about the basics of morality by accident, and the fault never lies entirely with their deceivers. Yes, someone may put out his foot to trip them—but they shut their eyes, pretend they don't see it, and take a fall. In such cases, the reminders and clarifications which ought to clear up the error don't work, and the reason is not that they are logically inadequate, but that the one who is deceived does not wish to be undeceived. The instant his rationalization for moral wrong has been exploded, lo, he has thought of another one. Its premises may be completely opposed to the premises of his previous rationalization, but this does not bother him; any port in a storm! In fact the "any port in a storm" sort of reasoning is so common in cases of willful confusion that it provides a rule of thumb for identifying them.

What the honestly confused person needs is a solution to his problems. What the willfully confused person needs is not a solution, but someone to call his bluff. One needs to see through him, and do it in such a way that even if only briefly, he sees through himself. Just for a moment his smokescreen has been blown away; caught by surprise, he has seen his reflection in the mirror. If he sees it once, there is always the chance that he will see it again. He will not forget that fleeting image. It will get under his skin. Perhaps some day when he is at lowest ebb, there will be a breakthrough. This is far less likely if he is a hardened advocate. Yet even if he does not see through himself, the audience may see through him, so even in this case his bluff should be called.

There is no fixed procedure for calling bluffs; it is an art. One cannot learn it from books. One can only become better through experience, as in cards. The first desideratum is to recognize *when* the other player is bluffing, *when* he not really confused but only playing at confusion—and that requires reflection on the things we can't not know.

— II —

Possible Futures

What will be required of us to welcome a
possible sanity and hold off a possible madness.

FOUR CHAPTERS AGO I quoted Chesterton's remark that men may keep a sort of level of good, but no man has ever been able to keep on one level of evil. We have seen that this is not a pious bromide but a literal truth, a small part of the law of natural consequences. Powerful forces are behind it, forces growing out of the design of the passions and the moral intellect.

What would it mean to give in to what is happening to us now? For we have gone very far already. Without a turning back, there can be only a going forward.

Having made our peace with forty million abortions, we will make our peace with forty million infanticides. As we begin to see already, there is no way to welcome the one without the other. If a fetus is not enough like an adult to be a "person," then neither is a babe in arms. If an unborn child is an "intruder" in the mother's womb, then a toddler is an intruder in her home. If an embryo is an "aggressor" against her liberty, then an infant is an aggressor against her heart. Adoption is good, but adoption will not solve the problem. If a pregnant mother can say

"I would *never* give up my baby"—yet kill him—then the mother or the father of a born child can do the same.

Having flirted with voluntary euthanasia, we will make it compulsory. Everywhere the former step has been taken, the latter has not long tarried; "mercy" has chained itself to terror. In the Netherlands, more than a tenth of elderly people who responded to a survey said that they feared being killed by their doctors without their consent;[1] thousands of people there carry cards in their pockets directing that if they are hospitalized, they do not want to be killed against their will. In the United States, if Oregon's approval of voluntary euthanasia has not been followed by other states, it is only because Oregon is premature; it acted too quickly to legalize what already went on quietly. The idea that life may be taken when doing so is "in the interests of all concerned" is already accepted in medical ethics circles. Social workers call it "helping families accept the reality of illness." People who do not want to die will feel obligated to die, to "spare their loved ones the burden." And think how much money it will save insurance companies.[2]

Having romanticized promiscuity, we will romanticize adultery. The trend is already well advanced in the movies, and no one spends money on a ticket unless he expects to be entertained; there is even historical precedent in the conventions of courtly love. Incest will come next; having embraced the ideology that the love which covers many sins is lust, we can hardly say no. Having smiled upon homosexuality, we will smile upon sodomy in all its forms. Anti-discrimination ordinances already forbid discrimination on grounds of generic "sexual preference"; what are pedophilia, bestiality, and necrophilia if not sexual preferences? Bestiality has been applauded by "the most influential ethicist alive."[3] Pedophilic themes have penetrated popular culture,[4] and articles in defense of sex with children are published in mainstream psychological journals.[5] Necrophilia cannot be far off, for it has already found a fashion niche: "Heroin chic" may have come and gone, but the ball it kicked into motion is still rolling. In what previous generation have young women preferred cosmetic tints that make their lips look like dead flesh?

Having separated sex from procreation, regarded pregnancy as an illness to be treated by drugs and knives,[6] and fused erotic enchantment with repulsion, we will rarely have children at all. The birthrate, already dropping, will plummet, and the "childfree" sensibility, already spreading, will become the norm. Fertility in eighty-three countries representing 44 percent of the world's population has fallen below replacement levels; in the developed countries, the net reproduction rate is 0.7 and dropping, which means that the next generation will be only 70% as large as this one.[7] Demographers are beginning to realize that the coming threat is not a population explosion, but a population implosion.[8] As the labor market shrinks, more women will be forced into the workplace, and fertility will drop more quickly still. As the population ages and the ration of workers to non-workers plunges, the pressure to kill old people will become even greater.

Having decided that human embryos are merely material for research purposes, we will find it impossible to resist so viewing other humans. Having harvested dying babies for their organs, we will begin to harvest dying adults; then we will make them die faster so that we can harvest them sooner. Biotechnology companies have already blended the ova of humans and pigs. As we saw in chapter three, one rationale is to escape ethical limits on the research use of human beings by using hybrids; but having made hybrids for research, we will make them for industry and entertainment.

Such a future may seem impossibly grim. But in all but material wealth, how we live now would once have seemed impossibly grim. Who in 1965 would have guessed that within a decade, abortion would be normalized; within three decades, homosexuality would be normalized; and within three and a half decades, biotechnicians would be crossing livestock with human beings?

This tableau is not a prediction. To predict human future is to deny human nature, for men and women are endowed with the perilous gift of free will. We can turn and go back the other way. Even so, free will does not mean that anything is possible. I cannot will that I shall do wrong, yet not be guilty. I cannot will that I shall be guilty, yet not suffer the impulsion to do further wrong. And I cannot will that I shall be unrepentant, yet stay the same.

It is a fearsome thing to recover sanity, almost as fearsome as not recovering it. For there are no half-measures in conscience; when the Furies loom behind you, there is no running in place. And so, to avoid travelling the next dark stretch of the road, there is no alternative but to make peace with the Furies, and travel back on the stretch we have lately come.

To set our faces against infanticide, we must repent abortion. To desist from viewing pregnancy as an illness, we must abjure viewing fertility as an ailment. To reprove perversion, we must repent lasciviousness. To turn from infidelity, we must forswear divorce and impurity. To withdraw from killing "in the interests of all concerned," we must rue the vain dream that our interests lie elsewhere than in innocence. To mourn treating the image of God as tissue to be harvested in hope of cures, we must sorrow over our sick fancy that there is nothing worse than physical disease. To turn back from the boundary of animal nature, we must repent that we defiled the sanctuary of human nature. To honor the inbuilt purposes of our design, we must honor the Designer who inbuilt them. And to honor the Designer, we must weep that we ever thought to take His place.

Whence comes the strength to do these things, to turn from tangled hopes and twisted visions, the Four Witnesses do not say. To that subject other witnesses must speak, and they have spoken, in thousands. It is said that the Designer Himself took the form of His designs, that He came into our night, that He wrought with the powers of darkness;

it is said that joy comes in the morning. To me this is more than rumor. I have been in the grip of those powers and I have known that dawn.

But even apart from this more-than-rumor, so much can be said: a kind of help, a lesser help, has been implanted in the very manner of our making. This too is part of the created order. If once the Turn is made, then just as there is a momentum to evil, so there is a momentum, not to virtue, but to repentance. As there is something in our design like Furies to drive us down, so there is something in our design like Angels to help us up. If it were not so, we could not even be told about it. Yet we can. The indestructibility of our longing for lightness, for purity, for music is like a small star of hope in a darkened sky, an inkling of the Star that rules the day.

APPENDICES

The Decalogue as a
Summary of the Natural Law

T HE TEN COMMANDMENTS, or Decalogue, were declared in both Exodus 20:2-17 and Deuteronomy 5:6-21. I am following the ordering of Deuteronomy, and using the traditional division and numbering. For Jews and Christians, the Decalogue derives paramount importance from the fact that it was expressly revealed by God. For natural law thinkers in general, when taken together with what it presupposes, implies, and suggests, it provides an unparalleled summary of those foundational moral principles which are both right for all and at some level known to all.

A slight complication is that the Decalogue was given to a particular nation in a particular time and place. For this reason, several of the Commandments express not only moral requirements which apply to everyone, but ceremonial requirements, which do not apply to everyone. Natural law thinkers focus on the former, not the latter. In the third commandment, for example, what draws their attention is that times must be set aside for the worship of God, not that the Hebrews were instructed to set aside the seventh day. For discussion, see Chapter 2.

FIRST TABLET OF THE DECALOGUE:
HONOR TO GOD AND HIS REPRESENTATIVES ON EARTH

1   I am the LORD your God, who brought you out of the land of Egypt, out of the house of bondage. You shall have no other gods before me. You shall not make for yourself a graven image, or any likeness of anything that is in heaven above, or that is on the earth beneath, or that is in the water under the earth; you shall not bow down to them or serve them; for I the LORD your God am a jealous God, visiting the iniquity of the fathers upon the children to the third and fourth generation of those who hate me, but showing steadfast love to thousands of those who love me and keep my commandments.

2   You shall not take the name of the LORD your God in vain: for the LORD will not hold him guiltless who takes his name in vain.

3   Observe the sabbath day, to keep it holy, as the LORD your God commanded you. Six days you shall labor, and do all your work; but the seventh day is a sabbath to the LORD your God; in it you shall not do any work, you, or your son, or your daughter, or your manservant, or your maidservant, or your ox, or your ass, or any of your cattle, or the sojourner who is within your gates, that your manservant and your maidservant may rest as well as you. You shall remember that you were a servant in the land of Egypt, and the LORD your God brought you out thence with a mighty hand and an outstretched arm; therefore the LORD your God commanded you to keep the sabbath day.

4   Honor your father and your mother, as the LORD your God commanded you; that your days may be prolonged, and that it may go well with you, in the land which the LORD your God gives you.

SECOND TABLET OF THE DECALOGUE:
HONOR TO ONE'S NEIGHBOR, AS GOD'S IMAGE

5   You shall not kill.

6   Neither shall you commit adultery.

7   Neither shall you steal.

8   Neither shall you bear false witness against your neighbor.

9   Neither shall you covet your neighbor's wife;

10 And you shall not desire your neighbor's house, his field, or his manservant, or his maidservant, his ox, or his ass, or anything that is your neighbor's.

SUMMARY

First Tablet (love God):

Hear, O Israel: The LORD our God is one LORD ; and you shall love the LORD your God with all your heart, and with all your soul, and with all your might.[1]

Second Tablet, first formulation (love neighbor as yourself):

You shall not hate your brother in your heart, but you shall reason with your neighbor, lest you bear sin because of him. You shall not take vengeance or bear any grudge against the sons of your own people, but you shall love your neighbor as yourself: I am the LORD.[2]

Second Tablet, second formulation (do unto others as yourself):

So whatever you wish that men would do to you, do so to them; for this is the law and the prophets.[3]

Both Tablets together:

And one of them, a lawyer, asked him a question, to test him. "Teacher, which is the great commandment in the law?" And he said to him, "You shall love the Lord your God with all your heart, and with all your soul, and with all your mind. This is the great and first commandment. And a second is like it, You shall love your neighbor as yourself. On these two commandments depend all the law and the prophets."[4]

The Noahide Commandments
as a Summary of the Natural Law

A CCORDING TO AN ANCIENT JEWISH TRADITION, to the Jews God gave the Torah, but to the "sons of Noah" He gave a shorter set of commandments. Insofar as the Noahide commandments are both right for all (the sons of Noah include everyone, both Jew and gentile) and at some level known to all (in some interpretations they are "written on the tablets of the heart"), they may be regarded as a Jewish summary of the natural law.

Torah includes 613 discrete commandments. Jewish commentators divide them into ten categories, with the Decalogue functioning not merely as a summary but as a classification scheme. In similar fashion, in Jewish tradition the sons of Noah are regarded as bound by a subset of these 613, divided into only seven categories, with the functions of summary and classification taken over by the Noahide Commandments.

Following is a brief statement of the seven commandments said to have been given to the sons of Noah. In italics I have correlated each commandment with the relevant article of the Decalogue, as I understand it.[1]

1   There must be provision for the administration of justice (as usually stated, courts). *Presupposed by Decalogue, Commandment Eight.*

2   There must be no idolatry. *Corresponds to Decalogue, Commandment One.*

3   There must be no blasphemy. *Corresponds to Decalogue, Commandment Two.*

4   There must be no sexual immorality. *Corresponds to Decalogue, Commandment Six, and, by extension, Commandment Nine, regarding them not only in the light of what they declare but in the light of what they suggest.*

5   There must be no bloodshed. *Corresponds to Decalogue, Commandment Five.*

6   There must be no theft. *Corresponds to Decalogue, Commandment Seven, and, by extension, Commandment Ten.*

7   There must be no eating of flesh torn from living animals. *Although this commandment does not correspond with any Commandment of the Decalogue, it would be universally accepted among natural law thinkers.*

Isaiah, David, and Paul
on the Natural Law

T HE NATURAL MEANS of attaining moral knowledge are four-fold: The witness of deep conscience, the witness of design as such, the witness of our own design, and the witness of natural consequences. Although few theories of natural law give equal attention to all four witnesses, all four of them are real.

A most interesting fact is that the Bible also testifies to their reality. Insights into the Four Witnesses pervade the scriptural text, sometimes appearing in unexpected places. This appendix does not attempt anything like an exhaustive inventory, but provides several striking examples.

ISAIAH 28:23-29

An oracle of the prophet Isaiah reads as follows.

[23]Give ear, and hear my voice; hearken, and hear my speech. [24]Does he who plows for sowing plow continually? does he continually open and harrow his ground? [25]When he has leveled its surface, does he not scatter dill, sow cummin, and put in wheat in rows and barley in its proper place, and spelt as the

border? [26]For he is instructed aright; his God teaches him. [27]Dill is not threshed with a threshing sledge, nor is a cart wheel rolled over cummin; but dill is beaten out with a stick, and cummin with a rod. [28]Does one crush bread grain? No, he does not thresh it for ever; when he drives his cart wheel over it with his horses, he does not crush it. [29]This also comes from the LORD of hosts; he is wonderful in counsel, and excellent in wisdom.

The gist of the passage is that the farmer knows all sorts of things—how long to plow, where to sow each kind of grain, how to separate each kind from the chaff—but all of his knowledge and technique comes from God. What could this mean?

Some people consider the passage a parable, comparing the way God tends his people to the way the farmer tends his crops. Considering the context in Isaiah, this is probably correct, but it does not explain in what sense God teaches the farmer to farm. The verb *yowrenu*, rendered "is instructed," means to chasten, discipline, or correct; its tense is imperfect, which in Hebrew usually indicates the future.[1] The verb *Wᵃyicrow*, rendered "teaches," means to point out, as if by aiming an arrow; its tense is perfect, which usually indicates the past but can also bear the timeless, "gnomic" sense it seems to carry here.[2] What it is that God points out is *lamishpaaT*, which means judgment or ordinance—the way things have been settled, as though in a court of law. So an idiomatic English rendering of "he is instructed aright; His God teaches him" might be "God will discipline the farmer; He is always pointing out to him how He has settled things." Two different modes of teaching are indicated.

I daresay that the passage would have been much more clear to Hebrew farmers than it is to us, because they experienced both modes every day. God calls the farmer's attention to how He has settled things by making the order of creation evident. Anyone can see that when seeds fall into the earth, they grow; anyone who pays attention can see that the different grains have different properties. In turn, He disciplines the farmer by having so arranged His creation that if the farmer is not attentive and does the wrong thing, it doesn't work. The crops do not come up, the grain does not separate from the chaff, the bread comes out wrong. In short, the farmer comes to understand his craft in two different ways: By reverently observing the design of God's creation, and by submitting to its inbuilt discipline. Taken together, these methods are so effective that eventually the farmer develops a second sense about growing things; he reads the soil, as the scholar reads his book. The wisdom of that part of creation which he tends has truly passed from his hands into his mind.

One can imagine a universe in which this sort of thing could not happen. Nature might have been so designed that the patterns of cause and effect were too elusive for human observation and too subtle and complex to be learned by trial and error. Or nature might have been designed without any cause and effect whatsoever. In such a world, neither method of instruction would work. But we have been placed in a different kind of world, a world which does have causal patterns, in which causes are an index to purposes, and in which the patterns of causality and purpose most important to human life are at just the right scale for us to learn them. Experience assists wisdom because the universe has been designed to make it so.

How things are meant to work is just plain enough to learn from observing them, and just simple enough to learn from the error of one's ways. This principle holds not only for the raising of crops but for the raising of all sorts of things—like families. The catch is that it works only in real life, not in the virtual life of books, which is one of the reasons that scholars can go so wrong.

PSALM 19

The bearing of Psalm 19 on our subject is almost too obvious to discuss. Suffice it to say that the poem is divided into three parts. In the first part, the psalmist, identified as David, calls attention to the witness of design in the physical order.

> [1]The heavens are telling the glory of God; and the firmament proclaims his handiwork.
> [2]Day to day pours forth speech, and night to night declares knowledge.
> [3]There is no speech, nor are there words; their voice is not heard;
> [4]Yet their voice goes out through all the earth, and their words to the end of the world. In them he has set a tent for the sun,
> [5]Which comes forth like a bridegroom leaving his chamber, and like a strong man runs its course with joy.
> [6]Its rising is from the end of the heavens, and its circuit to the end of them; and there is nothing hid from its heat.

The second part shifts focus, praising the design of the moral order; verse 11 alludes to the discipline of natural consequences.

> [7]The law of the LORD is perfect, reviving the soul; the testimony of the LORD is sure, making wise the simple;
> [8]the precepts of the LORD are right, rejoicing the heart; the commandment of the LORD is pure, enlightening the eyes;
> [9]the fear of the LORD is clean, enduring for ever; the ordinances of the LORD are true, and righteous altogether.
> [10]More to be desired are they than gold, even much fine gold; sweeter also than honey and drippings of the honeycomb.
> [11]Moreover by them is thy servant warned; in keeping them there is great reward.

In the third part the poet confesses our tendency to moral self-deception, and pleads for help.

¹²But who can discern his errors? Clear thou me from hidden faults.

¹³Keep back thy servant also from presumptuous sins; let them not have dominion over me! Then I shall be blameless, and innocent of great transgression.

¹⁴Let the words of my mouth and the meditation of my heart be acceptable in thy sight, O LORD, my rock and my redeemer.

ROMANS 1:18–2:16

The purpose of the first two chapters of St. Paul's letter to the young church in Rome is to demonstrate that although all have sinned and fallen short of the glory of God (3:23), no one can claim ignorance of God or His moral requirements as an excuse for doing so. Jews cannot claim ignorance, because they have the law of Moses and the Prophets; gentiles, because they have what I have called the Four Witnesses.

Paul comments vigorously on all four of them, beginning with the witness of design as such.

¹⁸For the wrath of God is revealed from heaven against all ungodliness and wickedness of men who by their wickedness suppress the truth. ¹⁹For what can be known about God is plain to them, because God has shown it to them. ²⁰Ever since the creation of the world his invisible nature, namely, his eternal power and deity, has been clearly perceived in the things that have been made. So they are without excuse; ²¹ᵃfor although they knew God they did not honor him as God or give thanks to him, . . .

He goes on to the witness of natural consequences: When we obstinately refuse to acknowledge the obvious, we become even stupider than we had intended to become.

[21b]. . . but they became futile in their thinking and their sense-less minds were darkened. [22]Claiming to be wise, they became fools, [23]and exchanged the glory of the immortal God for im-ages resembling mortal man or birds or animals or reptiles.

But obstinate stupidity has behavioral consequences too. The Scrip-tural writers do not always distinguish between what God brings about through the design of the natural order and what He brings about through intervention, because in both cases He is the cause. I believe, though, that in the following passage Paul is speaking of the former.

[24]Therefore God gave them up in the lusts of their hearts to im-purity, to the dishonoring of their bodies among themselves, [25]because they exchanged the truth about God for a lie and worshiped and served the creature rather than the Creator, who is blessed for ever! Amen. [26a]For this reason God gave them up to dishonorable passions.

His first example of dishonorable passion is homosexual lust, and his description of it brings in the witness of our own design, for he calls it *para phusein*—"against nature."

[26b]Their women exchanged natural relations for unnatural, [27]and the men likewise gave up natural relations with women and were consumed with passion for one another, men committing shameless acts with men and receiving in their own persons the due penalty for their error. [28]And since they did not see fit to acknowledge God, God gave them up to a base mind and to improper conduct.

I omit the next series of examples (a catalogue of vices) and skip to the first verse of the next chapter, where Paul restates the theme of his argument—that no one can claim ignorance of God and His moral requirements, and for that matter, no one can claim that he has fulfilled them.

> [1]Therefore you have no excuse, O man, whoever you are, when you judge another; for in passing judgment upon him you condemn yourself, because you, the judge, are doing the very same things. [2]We know that the judgment of God rightly falls upon those who do such things. [3]Do you suppose, O man, that when you judge those who do such things and yet do them yourself, you will escape the judgment of God? [4]Or do you presume upon the riches of his kindness and forbearance and patience? Do you not know that God's kindness is meant to lead you to repentance? [5]But by your hard and impenitent heart you are storing up wrath for yourself on the day of wrath when God's righteous judgment will be revealed.

The next series of verses emphasize that the preceding point applies to Jew and gentile alike, "for God shows no partiality" (verse 11). Paul's culminating evidence is deep conscience, which witnesses of God's moral requirements even to those outside Torah.

> [14]When Gentiles who have not the law [of Moses] do by nature what the law requires, they are a law to themselves, even though they do not have the law. [15]They show that what the law requires is written on their hearts, while their conscience also bears witness and their conflicting thoughts accuse or perhaps excuse them [16]on that day when, according to my gospel, God judges the secrets of men by Christ Jesus.

Paul uses the rest of the chapter to reemphasize the problem, and the next chapter to state the solution: We must rely, he says, not on our

own righteousness, but on the righteousness of the Savior, who takes
the burden of our sins upon Himself. Although this solution is of paramount importance, I comment no further on it here because it exceeds
my subject; it surpasses what can be known by the Four Witnesses alone.
Natural knowledge alone is sufficient to understand the "bad news" of
personal sin and rebellion. For the "good news" of a doorway back to
God, my faith points to the gospel.

An Example of Enmity to Nature:
The Redefinition of Pregnancy as a Disease

W HAT FOLLOWS is the conclusion of an article by Warren M. Hern, MD, "Is Pregnancy Really Normal?" *Family Planning Perspectives* 3:1 (January 1971), mentioned in chapter seven. I reproduce it here in full, first because ordinary people find it difficult to believe that such things could actually be written, second because the author claims that his opponents regularly misquote him (in his place, I would too). The full text of the article is available at the website of his abortion facility, <http://www.drhern.com>.

The foregoing discussion should allow us to abandon the erroneous assumption that pregnancy is per se a normal and desirable state, and to consider instead a more accurate view that human pregnancy is an episodic, moderately extended chronic condition with a definable morbidity and mortality risk to which females are uniquely though not uniformly susceptible and which:

- is almost entirely preventable through the use of effective contraception, and entirely so through abstinence;

- when not prevented, is the individual result of a set of species specific bio-social adaptations with a changing significance for species survival;

- may be defined as an illness requiring medical supervision through (a) cultural traditions, functional or explicit, (b) circumstantial self-definition of illness or (c) individual illness behavior;

- may be treated by evacuation of the uterine contents;

- may be tolerated, sought, and/or valued for the purpose of reproduction; and

- has an excellent prognosis for complete, spontaneous recovery if managed under careful medical supervision.

Accordingly, the open recognition and legitimation of pregnancy as an illness would be consistent with the individual self-interest of those experiencing pregnancy, good standards of medical practice, and the continued survival of human and other species.

Notes

Preface: Whom This Book Is For

1   David Novak, *The Image of the Non-Jew in Judaism: An Historical and Construc-
     tive Study of the Noachide Laws* (New York: Edwin Mellen, 1983), *Natural Law in
     Judaism* (Cambridge, England: Cambridge University Press, 1998), and *Covenantal
     Rights* (Princeton: Princeton University Press, 2000).

Introduction: The Moral Common Ground

1   Thomas Aquinas, *Summa Theologica*, 1-11, Question 94, Article 4.
2   Ibid., 41.
3   Ibid., 56.
4   Michael Ruse and E.O. Wilson, "The Evolution of Ethics," *New Scientist* 108:1478
     (17 October 1985): 50-52.
5   Shapiro was in turn quoting a letter to *The Wall Street Journal* by New York Uni-
     versity philosophy professor Peter Unger.
6   For snapshots of Singer's mind, see his articles "Killing Babies Isn't Always
     Wrong," in the September 16, 1995 edition of the London *Spectator* (20-22), and
     "Heavy Petting," a review of Midge Dekkers, trans. Paul Vincent, *Dearest Pet: On
     Bestiality,* in the March 1, 2001 edition of the online journal *Nerve.com* <http://
     www.nerve.com/Opinions/Singer/heavyPetting/>. The appointment of such as
     Singer is by no means unusual in academia. Unrepentant former Weather Un-

derground terrorists Bill Ayers and Bernadine Dohrn are faculty, respectively, in the School of Education, University of Illinois Chicago Campus, and the School of Law, Northwestern University. Ayers is a full professor; Dohrn is a clinical associate professor and the directory of the Children and Family Justice Center. A flattering New York Times profile of Ayers ("No Regrets for a Life of Explosives"), ironically published on the morning of the Al Qaeda attacks on the Pentagon and World Trade Center, quoted him as saying "I don't regret setting bombs. I feel we didn't do enough." He added that he would "not discount the possibility" of doing it again.

7   *Humanity: A Moral History of the Twentieth Century* (New Haven: Yale University Press, 2000; first published London: Jonathan Cape, 1999).

8   Especially Jonathan Glover, *Causing Death and Saving Lives* (New York: Penguin, 1977), and Jonathan Glover and others, *Ethics of New Reproductive Technologies: The Glover Report to the European Commission* (DeKalb: Northern Illinois University Press, 1989).

9   "When Gentiles who have not the law [of Moses] do by nature what the law requires, they are a law to themselves, even though they do not have the law. They show that what the law requires is written on their hearts, while their conscience also bears witness and their conflicting thoughts accuse or perhaps excuse them[.]" (Romans 2:14-15, RSV.)

10 In a certain special sense, of the rest of nature too—but this point requires more explanation, and will be taken up later.

1 Things We Can't Not Know

1   John M. Cooper, "The Relations Between Religion and Morality in Primitive Culture," cited in Heinrich A. Rommen, trans. Thomas R. Hanley, intro. Russell Hittinger, *The Natural Law: A Study in Legal and Social Philosophy and History* (Indianapolis: Liberty Fund, 1998, orig. 1946), 201, note 18.

2   See Gregory A. Boyd, *God at War* (Downers Grove, Penn.: InterVarsity Press, 1997), 119-29, esp. 124-26.

3   *Planned Parenthood v. Casey,* 505 U.S. 833 (1992), 851.

2 What It Is We Can't Not Know

1   See especially *Summa Theologica* I-II, Question 100.

2   The Bible declares the Ten Commandments in two different places, and how to divide them into ten is not specified in either one. Of the two divisions in common use, I follow Augustine's, employed by all Catholics and some Protestants. Other Protestants employ a division found in Philo, Josephus, and Origen, which

splits the first commandment into two but combines the last two commandments into one. I also follow the wording of Deuteronomy 5:6-21 rather than Exodus 20:2-17. The wording is nearly identical, and in both the same things are commanded. However, they attach different remarks to the commandment to set aside a day of rest, and in the concluding verse, Deuteronomy reverses the order in which coveting one's neighbor's wife and coveting one's neighbor's house are listed.

3   *Summa Theologica,* I-II, Question 100, Article 3, esp. the replies to the first and fourth objections.

4   He goes on to say of the pagans, "So they are without excuse; for although they knew God they did not honor him as God or give thanks to him, but they became futile in their thinking and their senseless minds were darkened." Romans 1:20-21, RSV.

5   Deuteronomy adds, "You shall remember that you were a servant in the land of Egypt, and the LORD your God brought you out thence with a mighty hand and an outstretched arm; therefore the LORD your God commanded you to keep the sabbath day" — emphasizing that servants too are to be given their intermission. After the same Commandment, Exodus adds, "for in six days the LORD made heaven and earth, the sea, and all that is in them, and rested the seventh day; therefore the LORD blessed the sabbath day and hallowed it"—emphasizing that the intermission honors God for what He has done in creation. Six days we honor Him by laboring in the created world; one day we honor him by contemplating the created world as His labor.

6   See, for example, Thomas Aquinas, *Summa Theologica* I-II, Question 100, Article 7, Reply to Objection 5.

7   Sara McLanahan and Gary Sandefur, *Growing Up with a Single Parent: What Hurts, What Helps* (Cambridge: Harvard University Press, 1994), 38.

8   *Strong's Concordance,* "properly, to dash in pieces, i.e. kill (a human being), especially to murder"; *Brown, Driver, and Briggs' Hebrew Lexicon,* "to murder, to slay, to kill."

9   David T. Lykken, *The Antisocial Personality* (Hillsdale, NJ: Lawrence Erlbaum Associates, 1995), 28.

10 Though not a proponent of natural law, Lykken prefaces the story by remarking, "It is an interesting and important fact that most of the diverse criminal types suggested here do tend to justify their conduct in one way or another, at least to themselves." Ibid.

11 The question is *not* whether the intent to deceive *as such* is always wrong. My answer would be "no."

12 Matthew 22:37b-40. The two branches of this summary are also stated or implied in the following places, among others. The first: Deuteronomy 6:5, 11:1, 11:13, 13:3, and 30:6, Joshua 22:5 and 23:11, Psalm 31:23, Mark 12:30, and Luke 10:27. The sec-

ond: Leviticus 19:18, Matthew 19:19, Mark 12:31, Luke 10:27 (as amplified by Luke 10:29-37), Romans 13:8-10, Galatians 5:14, and James 2:8.

13   Luke 6:31; see also Matthew 7:12.

14   He adds "either through nature or through faith," but we have already seen that Thomas views faith and reasoning as complements, not opposites.

15   1 John 4:19-21.

16   1 John 5:2-3.

3 Could We Get By Knowing Less?

1   John Rawls, *Political Liberalism* (New York: Columbia University Press, 1993).

2   This is not contradicted by the biblical doctrine of the fall. A crushed foot does not thereby become a hand; the proposition that we are in conflict with our nature is quite different from the proposition that it is not, in fact, our nature.

3   Paraphrasing paleontologist George Gaylord Simpson, a neo-Darwinist: "The meaning of evolution is that man is the result of a purposeless and natural process that did not have us in mind." *The Meaning of Evolution*, rev. ed. (New Haven: Yale University Press, 1967), 344-45.

4   J. Bottum, "The Pig-Man Cometh," *The Weekly Standard* (October 23, 2000) © News America Incorporated).

5   *De Jure Belli ac Pacis*, Book 3, Prolegomena, paragraph 11.

6   I am paraphrasing the formal characterization of purpose offered by Robert C. Koons: "type A occurs in context C for purpose B if and only if, whenever a token of type (A & C) occurs, it is most probably caused, in part, by the fact that A-tokens tend to cause B-tokens." See Koons, "Higher-Order Causation: A Situation-Theoretic Account," *Mind and Machines*, Vol. 8, (1998), 559-85, as well as Koons, *Realism Regained: An Exact Theory of Causation, Teleology, and the Mind* (New York: Oxford University Press, 2000).

7   Richard Swinburne elaborates an argument something like this in *The Existence of God* (Oxford: Oxford University Press, 1979).

8   Richard Lewontin, "Billions and Billions of Demons" *New York Review of Books* 44:1 (January 9, 1997): 28-32.

9   Thomas Nagel, *The Last Word* (Oxford: Oxford University Press, 1996), 130-31.

10   Compare *Humanist Manifesto II* (1973), which declared in its first principle that "we can discover no divine purpose or providence for the human species. While there is much that we do not know, humans are responsible for what we are or will become. No deity will save us; we must save ourselves." In Paul Kurtz, *Humanist Manifestos I and II* (New York: Prometheus Books, 1973).

11   This section incorporates a portion of my essay "Thou Shalt Not Kill—Whom?

The Meaning of the Person," presented at the 2002 meeting of the American Political Science Association and forthcoming in Robert P. George, ed., *Law and Persons* (Princeton, New Jersey: Princeton University Press).

12 Mary Ann Warren, "On the Moral and Legal Status of Abortion," *The Monist* 57:4 (1973).

13 Mary Ann Warren, "Postscript on Infanticide," in Sue Dwyer and Joel Feinberg, eds. *The Problem of Abortion*, 3d ed. (Belmont, California: Wadsworth Publishing, 1997), 71-74.

14 "I've always been a classic liberal. I believe in freedom in its broadest sense .... I frankly think the soul or personage comes in when the fetus is accepted by the mother." Abortionist James McMahon, as quoted in "The Abortions of Last Resort: The Question of Ending Pregnancy in Its Later Stages May Be the Most Anguishing of the Entire Abortion Debate," *Los Angeles Times Magazine,* 7 February 1990, cited in Faith Abbott, "The Abortionist as Craftsman," reprinted in *Human Life Review* 22:1 (Winter, 1996), 23-34, at 24. "In my opinion a foetus is not a person in the way a woman is. Personhood is conferred by the woman giving birth. It is an act." Retired abortionist David Paintin, as quoted in Nicci Gerrard, with Kim Bunce and Kirsty Buttfield, "Damned If You Do . . .", *The Observer* (22 April 2001), webbed at <http://www.observer.co.uk/review/story/0,6903,476313,00.html>.

4 The First and Second Witnesses

1 "In past generations he allowed all the nations to walk in their own ways; yet he did not leave himself without witness, for he did good and gave you from heaven rains and fruitful seasons, satisfying your hearts with food and gladness" (Acts 14:16-17, RSV).

2 This is a late Greek word related to *syneidesis,* an older word used by the New Testament for conscience. The first syllable is pronounced not "sin" but "soon."

3 Latin.

4 Compare Thomas Aquinas, *Summa Theologica* 1-11, Question 94, Articles 4 & 6.

5 It may seem that friendship is not one of the inviolables, because if my friend asks me to do wrong I should refuse. But loyalty to my friend does not mean that I will do everything he asks; it means that I will never act against his true good or the moral integrity of our relationship.

6 Gerrard, *supra,* Chapter 2.

7 *The Selfish Gene* (Oxford: Oxford University Press, 1989), Preface to the 1976 edition.

8 Dawkins, 3.

9   Neo-Darwinian paleontologist George Gaylord Simpson, *The Meaning of Evolution*, rev. ed. (New Haven: Yale University Press, 1967), 344-45.

10 Michael J. Behe, *Darwin's Black Box: The Biochemical Challenge to Evolution* (New York: The Free Press, 1997). For a brief account see Behe, "Evidence for Intelligent Design from Biochemistry," posted to the internet at <http://www.arn.org/docs/behe/mb_idfrombiochemistry.htm>.

11 Charles Darwin, *The Origin of Species*, 6th ed. (1872), Chapter 6; in the 1988 edition of New York University Press, 154.

12 Fred Hoyle, "The Universe: Past and Present Reflections," *Annual Review of Astronomy and Astrophysics* 20 (1982), 1-35, at 16.

13 George Wald, "The Origin of Life", *Scientific American* 191:48 (May 1954).

14 In previous works I have sometimes described this as a fifth witness, the witness of Godward longing. Simply as a longing, however, it has no independent cognitive status. It seems more accurate to think of it as a true intuition of God as creator, an intuition which *gives rise* to a longing for its object.

15 A famous humanist document of 1933 declares that "In place of the old attitudes involved in worship and prayer the humanist finds his religious emotions expressed in a heightened sense of personal life and in a cooperative effort to promote social well being. ... It follows that there will be no uniquely religious emotions and attitudes of the kind hitherto associated with belief in the supernatural." Paul Kurtz, *supra*, Chapter 3.

16 See esp. Edward O. Wilson, *On Human Nature* (Cambridge, Mass.: Harvard University Press, 1978). In his more recent *Consilience: The Unity of Knowledge* (New York: Knopf, 1998), he proposes various other ways in which belief in God might have selective advantage, all with the same defect.

17 *No Free Lunch: Why Specified Complexity Cannot Be Purchased without Intelligence* (Lanham, Maryland: Rowman and Littlefield, 2001), chapter 6, "Design as a Scientific Research Program"; more briefly, "Design as a Research Program: 14 Questions to Ask About Design" (13 June 2000), published on the internet at <http://www.discovery.org/viewDB/index.php3?program=CRSC%20Responses&command=view&id=259>.

5 *The Third and Fourth Witnesses*

1   Sometimes this is even said consciously. When a homosexual performance artist in my home city consumed human ashes on the stage, the meaning was obvious: "Death, I take you into me."

2   See the remarks of St. Paul in Romans 12:1-8.

3   This point has been best articulated by Robert P. George, most recently in *The*

Clash of Orthodoxies: Law, Religion, and Morality in Crisis (Wilmington, Delaware: ISI Books, 2001). See esp. the chapter on marriage and neutrality.

4 For a more precise account of these matters, see William A. Dembski, *The Design Inference: Eliminating Chance Through Small Probabilities* (Cambridge, England: Cambridge University Press, 1998).

5 Edmund Burke, *Reflections on the French Revolution,* Everyman ed. (London: J.M. Dent & Sons, 1955), 44.

6 Paraphrasing René König, "Sociological Introduction [to the family]," *International Encyclopedia of Comparative Law* (1974), Volume IV:1, 42-43.

7 G.K. Chesterton, "On Certain Modern Writers and the Institution of the Family," *Heretics* (1905). In *Collected Works of G.K. Chesterton* (San Francisco: Ignatius Press, 1986-), Volume 1.

8 Pius XI, *Quadragesimo Anno* (English title: "On Reconstruction of the Social Order"), May 15, 1931, Section 79.

9 *Summa Theologica* I-II, Question 95, Article 1.

10 Galatians 6:7.

11 For St. Thomas's discussion of some of these natural penalties (and some others besides), see *Summa Contra Gentiles,* esp. the chapters "Of the Reason for Which Simple Fornication is a Sin by Divine Law, and of the Natural Institution of Marriage" and "That Marriage Ought to be Indissoluble."

12 Of the two different ways of "deriving" human law from natural law, this example corresponds to the second—not the one St. Thomas calls "conclusion from premises" (as we would say, deduction), but the one he calls "determination of certain generalities" (as we would say, filling in the blanks). The first mode of derivation accounts for the common features of all good systems of human law, while the second accounts for their differences. This distinction is found in *Summa Theologica,* Question 95, Article 2.

13 Thomas Aquinas, *Summa Theologica* I-II, Question 96, Article 2; compare Question 91, Article 4.

14 Part 1, Chapter 14.

15 "For there is no such *finis ultimus* (utmost aim) nor *summum bonum* (greatest good) as is spoken of in the books of the old moral philosophers" (Part 1, Chapter 22).

16 "The right of nature, which writers commonly call *jus naturale,* is the liberty each man hath to use his own power as he will himself for the preservation of his own nature; that is to say, of his own life; and consequently, of doing anything which, in his own judgement and reason, he shall conceive to be the aptest means thereunto" (Part 1, Chapter 14).

17 See John Finnis, *Natural Law and Natural Rights* (Oxford: Oxford University Press, 1980), and Germain G. Grisez, *The Way of the Lord Jesus,* 3 vols. (Quincy,

Illinois: Franciscan Press, 1983-1997). For a shorter treatment, see Germain G. Grisez, John Finnis, and Joseph M. Boyle, "Practical principles, moral truth, and ultimate ends," *American Journal of Jurisprudence* 32 (1987), 99-151.

18   See Chapter 2.

6 *Some Objections*

1   I do borrow a few sentences from them.
2   In the theory of intelligent design, this is called running the patterns through the explanatory filter. See William A. Dembski, cited in Chapter 5; also Dembski, *Intelligent Design: The Bridge Between Science and Theology* (Downers Grove, Illinois: InterVarsity, 1999).
3   Chapter 4.
4   Chapter 4.
5   Concerning the tendency of sociopaths to justify their behavior to themselves, see Chapter 2, note 10.
6   I return to this theme in Chapter 9, where I discuss it at greater length.
7   *Restatement of Contracts,* 1932, Section 90.
8   See also Appendix 3.
9   Romans 2:14-15 (RSV).
10   Galatians 6:7 (RSV).
11   Acts 17:22-23.
12   Romans 1:18-19.
13   For example Proverbs 1:7, 1:32, 15:14.
14   *Humanist Manifesto II,* proposition three. In Paul Kurtz, *supra,* Chapter 3.

7 *Denial*

1   1 Timothy 4:2.
2   Mary Meehan, "The Ex-Abortionists: Why They Quit," *Human Life Review* 26:2-3 (Spring-Summer 2000), 8.
3   Wendy Simonds, Charlotte Ellertson, Kimberly Springer, and Beverley Winikoff, "Abortion, Revised: Participants in the U.S. Clinical Trials Evaluate Mifepristone," *Social Science and Medicine* 46:10 (1998): 1316.
4   Ibid., 1318-1319.
5   Ibid., 1317.
6   Warren M. Hern, M.D., "Is Pregnancy Really Normal?" *Family Planning Perspectives* 3:1 (January 1971). In a telephone call to my home on 14 December 2001 after I had called his abortion facility to request another of his articles, Dr. Hern bitterly complained that abortion opponents "regularly misquote me." I therefore

reproduce the entire conclusion of the article in Appendix 4. The full text is posted at his website, <http://www.drhern.com>.

7   Meehan, op. cit., p. 19.

8   Three-quarters of the respondents in a national survey of college women define "hooking up" as "when a girl and a guy get together for a physical encounter [anything from kissing to sexual intercourse] and don't necessarily expect anything further." Four in ten said they had hooked up; one in ten that they had done so more than six times. Eight in ten considered marriage a "very important" life goal, although this hardly seems a good way to find a husband. Norval Glenn and Elizabeth Marquardt, et. al., "Hooking Up, Hanging Out, and Hoping for Mr. Right—College Women on Dating and Mating Today," survey conducted for the Independent Women's Forum by the Institute for American Values, webbed at <http://www.iwf.org/news/010727.shtml>.

9   George E. DeLury, *But What If She Wants to Die? A Husband's Diary* (Secaucus, N.J.: Birch Lane Press/Carol Publishing Group, 1997), 178-79, omitting paragraph divisions.

10   Ibid., 145.

11   Susan Cheever, "An Act of Mercy? A Memoir by a Husband Who Helped His Ailing Wife to Die," *The New York Times on the Web* (20 July 1997), posted at <http://times.com/books/97/07/20/reviews/970720.cheever.html>.

12   Psalm 51:14,16-17 (RSV).

13   Micah 6:6-8 (RSV).

14   Christianity regards this as literally true, so that penitents must rely not on the rags of their own righteousness but on the perfect righteousness of Christ.

15   Ginette Paris, *The Sacrament of Abortion,* trans. Joanna Mott (Dallas: Spring Publications, 1992), 92, 107.

16   Simonds et. al., 1319.

17   Simonds et. al., 1320-1321.

18   Quoted in Mary Meehan, op. cit., 12.

19   Fyodor Dostoyevsky, in a letter to the prospective publisher of what became *Crime and Punishment*; quoted by Ernest J. Simmons, "Introduction," *Crime and Punishment* (New York: Dell, 1959), 12.

20   Herbert Hendin, M.D., *Seduced by Death: Doctors, Patients, and the Dutch Cure* (New York: W.W. Norton, 1997), 222.

21   John Thomas Noonan, *A Private Choice* (New York: The Free Press, 1979), 82.

22   Senator Rick Santorum (R-Pa.): "But I would like to ask you this question. You agree, once the child is born, separated from the mother, that that child is protected by the Constitution and cannot be killed? Do you agree with that?" Senator Barbara Boxer (D-Ca.): "I would make this statement. That this Constitution as it currently is—some want to amend it to say life begins at conception. I think

when you bring your baby home, when your baby is born—and there is no such thing as partial-birth—the baby belongs to your family and has the rights." *Congressional Record,* 20 October 1999, page s12878. See also Chapter 9 of this book.

23 Joseph Smaylor, ed., *Gleanings from Johnson* (London: Wells, Gardner, Darton, and Co., 1899), 76.

24 Henry Wadsworth Longfellow, *Michael Angelo.*

25 Eileen L. McDonagh: "Some might suggest that the solution to coercive pregnancy is simply for the woman to wait until the fetus is born, at which point its coercive imposition of pregnancy will cease. This type of reasoning is akin to suggesting that a woman being raped should wait until the rape is over rather than stopping the rapist." Eileen L. McDonagh, *Breaking the Abortion Deadlock: From Choice to Consent* (Oxford: Oxford University Press, 1996), 11-12. What McDonagh means by a "coercive" pregnancy is "what the fertilized ovum does to a woman when it makes her pregnant without her consent," 7.

26 Ibid., 192.

27 See Chapter 3.

28 He puts the remark in the mouth of the hero in "The Flying Stars." See G.K. Chesterton, *The Penguin Complete Father Brown* (New York: Penguin, 1981), 63.

29 It might even be supposed that to raise them such a God would die for them; Christianity claims that He actually has, although natural law by itself knows nothing of such things.

8 *Eclipse*

1 This subsection substantially follows Ralph McInerny, "Are There Moral Truths That Everyone Knows?", in Edward B. McLean, ed., *Common Truths: New Perspectives on Natural Law* (Wilmington, Delaware: ISI Books, 2000). I am solely responsible for any absurdities.

2 The infamous "mystery passage" of *Planned Parenthood v. Casey,* 505 U.S. 833 (1992), at 851.

3 Webbed at <http://www.figures.com/Features/index.html?show_article=22313& domain=figures.com&dom=fig&domain_id=4>.

4 Robert Christgau, "Consumer Guide: Getting Them Straight," *The Village Voice* (16-22 August 2000). Webbed at <http://www.villagevoice.com/issues/0033/ christgau.php>.

5 From an interview with Stott in Albert Y. Hsu, *Singles at the Crossroads* (Downers Grove, Illinois: InterVarsity Press, 1997), 181.

6 John Keats, Letter to Benjamin Bailey, 22 November 1817.

7 Lynn Grabhorn, *Excuse Me, Your Life is Waiting: The Astonishing Power of Feelings* (Charlottesville, VA: Hampton Roads Publishing, 2000), back cover.

8   C.S. Lewis, *That Hideous Strength* (New York: Macmillan, 1946), 268-69.

9   Steven Pinker, "Why They Kill Their Newborns," *The New York Times Magazine*, 1 November 1997; emphasis added.

10 Hannibal Lecter is the cannibalistic aesthete of the Thomas Harris novels *Silence of the Lambs* and *Hannibal*, better known in their movie versions.

11 John Keats, Letter to Benjamin Bailey, 22 November 1817.

12 Neale Donald Walsch, *Conversations With God*, Vol. 1 (New York: G.P. Putnam's Sons, 1995), quotations from 4, 5, 83, and 26, in that order. Here, roughly, is how Walsch's argument for his own godhood runs: (1) God is the greatest entity imaginable. (2) So God is All Things. (3) Naturally, All Things has no consciousness of its own. (4) So God can experience itself as God only through parts of itself that do have consciousness. (5) That's you and me. (6) But All Things is all there is. (7)So there's really only one thing. (8) So we drop the distinction between All and its parts. (9) So we're not just parts of God—we're God. (10) But there is only one of us. (11) So God is Me.

13 Wilson, *The Moral Sense*, 100.

14 Ibid., 79.

9 *The Public Relations of Moral Wrong*

1   G.K. Chesterton, *Eugenics and Other Evils* (1922), Chapter 3, "The Anarchy From Above." In *Collected Works of G.K. Chesterton* (San Francisco: Ignatius Press, 1986), Volume 4.

2   C.S. Lewis, *The Abolition of Man* (New York: Macmillan, 1947, 1955), pp. 54-56. Lewis did not say that the subjects of these two examples were Communism and Fascism, but I think their identity is plain.

3   Not to be confused with the "belt" of deep conscience, discussed in Chapter 4; that pertains to knowledge, whereas this pertains to emotions and desires.

4   *Congressional Record* (20 October 1999), s12879.

5   Eileen McDonagh, *supra*, 36.

6   Ginette Paris, *supra*, 53 and 27, in order.

7   Robert Jay Lifton, *supra*.

8   Tom Segev, *Soldiers of Evil: The Commandants of the Nazi Concentration Camps*, trans. Haim Watzman (New York: McGraw-Hill, 1987), 80.

9   Gitta Sereny, *Into That Darkness: An Examination of Conscience* (New York: Vintage Books, 1983 [1974]), 101.

10 Warren M. Hern and Billie Corrigan, Boulder Abortion Clinic, Boulder, Colorado, "What About Us? Staff Reactions to D & E," presented at the 1978 meeting of the Association of Planned Parenthood Physicians, San Diego, California, October 26, published in *Advances in Planned Parenthood* 15:1 (1980), 3-8.

11 Ibid.

12 Hitler practiced the technique even while pretending to condemn it. Here is the passage, from *Mein Kampf,* Vol. I, Chap. 10: "[T]he magnitude of a lie always contains a certain factor of credibility, since the great masses of the people in the very bottom of their hearts tend to be corrupted rather than consciously and purposely evil, and that, therefore, in view of the primitive simplicity of their minds they more easily fall a victim to a big lie than to a little one, since they themselves lie in little things, but would be ashamed of lies that were too big. Such a falsehood will never enter their heads and they will not be able to believe in the possibility of such monstrous effrontery and infamous misrepresentation in others; yes, even when enlightened on the subject, they will long doubt and waver, and continue to accept at least one of these causes as true. Therefore, something of even the most insolent lie will always remain and stick—a fact which all the great lie-virtuosi and lying-clubs in this world know only too well and also make the most treacherous use of."

10 *The Public Relations of Moral Right*

1   Susan B. Anthony, *The Revolution* 4:1 (8 July 1869), p. 4.

2   Eileen McDonagh, *supra*, 6, 22, 76, 176, 188, 192.

3   Paul Weyrich, "The Moral Minority," in the colloquium "Is the Religious Right Finished?," *Christianity Today* (6 September 1999), webbed at <http://www.christianitytoday.com/ct/9ta/9ta043.html>.

4   Fundamentalists differ from other doctrinally conservative Christians not in their beliefs but in their reluctant approach to engagement with the surrounding culture.

5   Romans 12:2 (NIV).

6   Isaiah 45:1-4; Ezra 1 (entire).

7   McDonagh, op. cit., p. 82. 246

8   Ibid., p. 192.

9   *The Journal of Homosexuality* 20:1&2 (1990), "Male Intergenerational Intimacy: Historical, Socio-Psychological, and Legal Perspectives."

11 *Possible Futures*

1   Richard Miniter, "The Dutch Way of Death," *Opinion Journal* (28 April 2001).

2   See Wesley J. Smith, *Culture of Death: The Assault on Medical Ethics in America* (San Francisco: Encounter Books, 2001).

3   See Introduction.

4   Mary Eberstadt, "Pedophilia Chic Reconsidered." *The Weekly Standard* 6:16 (8 January 2001).

5   Bruce Rind, Philip Tromovitch, and Robert Bauserman, "A Meta-analytic Examination of Assumed Properties of Child Sexual Abuse Using College Samples." *Psychological Bulletin* 124:1 (July 1998), 22-53. *Psychological Bulletin* is published by the American Psychological Association.

6   See Appendix 4.

7   Although fertility levels in the United States are higher than in Europe, the trend is downward here as well.

8   See Nicholas Eberstadt, "World Population Implosion? Speculations About the Demographics of De-population," *The Public Interest* (Fall 1997), "The Population Implosion," *Foreign Policy* (March 2001).

APPENDIX 1

1   Deuteronomy 6:4-5, RSV; compare Deuteronomy 11:1, 11:13-14, 30:6, and Joshua 22:5.

2   Leviticus 19:17-18, RSV; compare Matthew 19:18-19, Romans 13:8-10, Galatians 5:14, and James 2:8.

3   Matthew 7:12, RSV; compare Luke 6:31-33.

4   Matthew 22:35-40, RSV; compare Mark 12:28-31 and Luke 10:25-28 (as amplified by Luke 10:29-37).

APPENDIX 2

1   An outstanding study of the Noahide Commandments from a Jewish perspective can be found in David Novak, *The Image of the Non-Jew in Judaism: An Historical and Constructive Study of the Noahide Laws* (New York: Edwin Mellen, 1983). For a brief discussion, see my *Written on the Heart: The Case for Natural Law* (Downers Grove: InterVarsity Press, 1997), 202-207.

APPENDIX 3

1   I am indebted to the Rev. Dr. William A. Dickson for deciphering the Hebrew verb tenses for me. Any error is my own.

2   All three verbs in the final sentence are also perfect.

Index

J. Budziszewski is professor of government and philosophy at the University of Texas. He is the author of *The Revenge of Conscience: Politics and the Fall of Man*, *Written on the Heart: The Case for Natural Law*, and *How to Stay Christian in College*.

This book was designed and set into type
by Mitchell S. Muncy,
with cover design by Sam Torode,
and printed and bound
by Edwards Brothers, Inc.,
Ann Arbor, Michigan.

❧

The text face is Adobe Caslon,
designed by Carol Twombly,
based on faces cut by William Caslon, London, in the 1730s,
and issued in digital form by Adobe Systems,
Mountain View, California, in 1989.

❧

The paper is acid-free and is of archival quality.

 33